On-Target Learning

On-Target Learning

Redefining Organizational Learning

Daniel R. Tobin

Copyright © 2019 Daniel R. Tobin

All rights reserved

ISBN 9781092826723

Table of Contents

Introduction	1
Chapter 1: Failing to Make the Grade	7
Chapter 2: The Learning Contract Part I	21
Chapter 3: The Learning Contract Part II	76
Chapter 4: The Learning Contract Part III	142
Chapter 5: Evaluating Your Learning Initiatives	156
Chapter 6: Other Lessons Learned	171
Books by Dan Tobin	200
About Dan Tobin	201

Introduction

In the mid-1990s, I was looking for a new job. I had been contacted by a headhunter about a position as North American training director for a global software company. After lengthy discussions with the headhunter, he told me that I was a great candidate and that he would present my qualifications to the hiring manager the next morning. My hopes were high.

The next afternoon, the headhunter called. "The hiring manager remembered you from your years working at Digital Equipment Corporation (DEC)," he told me. He also told me that the hiring manager had called me "a major disruptor" and said that I "had a lot to answer for in terms of my work at DEC." I had spent 11 years working at DEC and, yes, I could be viewed as "a major disruptor" of the company's educational services organization (I will give examples of this throughout the book). But I was also very proud of the work I had done there and how it had contributed to the success of the company's business.

I asked him for the name of the hiring manager. Let's call him John. John had been a senior manager in DEC's educational services organization for more than 20 years. He was one of the architects of the organization's written-in-stone methodology for training. Whenever I had suggested a new idea or a new method for the training programs I managed, those ideas always seemed to work their way up to John's desk, and his response was always the same: "That's not the way we do things." Then he would hand me a copy of the 4-inch binder that detailed the educational services methodology, starting with how to write a question for a needs assessment to what font style and size to use in student materials.

When I protested that the standard methodology would not meet the needs of the business I was supporting, I always got the same response: "This is how we do things – live with it." And when I went around him and his methodology to create some of the most impactful programs the company had ever seen, he did everything he could to subvert my efforts. In fact, he never forgave me for succeeding.

I told the headhunter some of this history and told him to tell John what he could do with the job.

Note: To be fair, DEC's educational services organization did a lot of great work. They regularly won awards for the quality of their training materials and they were pioneers in e-learning – in the early

1980s, they created the Interactive Video Instructional System (IVIS), which predated PCs and other types of computer-based learning, using a programmed video disk system.

I have worked in the training and development field for almost 40 years. Actually, if I broaden that to the "learning" field, I have been at it for 50 years, having started my full-time working life as a junior high school math teacher after graduating from college. During this time, I have worked in several companies as a one-person training department, founded two corporate universities, served as Vice President of Program Design and Development for the American Management Association, consulted to companies across the United States, and given keynotes and workshops on five continents.

Throughout my career, I have been regarded as an innovator and a disruptor (as attested to by John). Many of the learning solutions I have developed and which at the time seemed simple and logical to me, have surprisingly (to me) seemed to be revelations to others. Perhaps because my formal education was not in instructional design, I didn't feel hemmed in by the methodologies of that field. I have often questioned the *status quo*, and often been disdained for doing so. But I have also had some great successes.

Perhaps I can best explain my approach to organizational learning by drawing the distinction between "educational research" and "policy research." When I was working on my Ph.D. in the economics of education at Cornell University, I took courses to learn the methodologies of my field. When I took my oral examinations, I was tested on how well I had mastered those methodologies. And when I researched and wrote my dissertation, the measure was not so much the results of my research but whether I had correctly applied the research methodologies. These are the requirements of educational research – to learn and to correctly apply the methodologies of your field, no matter if the field is education, economics, history, or engineering – adherence to methodology is of prime importance.

Policy research is different. With policy research, a decision maker might say, "I've got to make a decision on this issue two weeks from now. I want you to do as much research as you can in that time so that I can make the best, most informed decision possible." It is not that methodology isn't important in policy research, but that making a timely decision is more important.

I would argue that corporate training groups have generally relied too heavily on the educational research model when what is needed is a greater emphasis on making timely decisions to support the organization's business goals.

Over the course of my career, I have built an outstanding "personal learning network" (PLN). Through people I have worked for and with, through consulting and speaking engagements around the world, through people I have met at conferences, and through the research I have done for my seven previous books on corporate learning strategies, I have collected dozens, if not hundreds, of "excellent practices." I don't like to use the term "best practices" because what is "best" for one company or situation is often not the best for others. I have learned from many excellent practitioners and I am grateful to each and every one of them.

I have written this book with two purposes in mind. First, over the past 20 years, I have presented to many training and human resources conferences my model for what I call a "Learning Contract." The Learning Contract is a process to ensure that all learning initiatives within an organization are tied directly to that organization's business goals, AND that what is learned is actually applied to people's work to make a positive difference in the achievement of organizational, group, and individual goals. This is what I mean by the term "On-Target Learning" – where the target is business results. The Learning Contract is the subject of Chapters 1 through 4. Chapter 5 deals with the always controversial topic of how to evaluate the results of your learning initiatives.

The second purpose of the book is to share many of my experiences as a training manager and consultant. As I said earlier, I have found that many of the ideas I have found to be logical and simple have, surprisingly to me, been revelations to others.

So, I hope to pass along some of my experience and, hopefully, the wisdom I have developed over the past 50 years in Chapter 6.

Now semi-retired (except for the occasional consulting assignment or speaking engagement), my hope is that everyone who reads this book will find at least a few ideas that can help them improve the efforts of their training groups and that every reader will benefit from what I consider my legacy to the training/learning/talent development field.

Chapter 1

Failing to Make the Grade: The Need to Redefine Organizational Learning

I often start presentations to training groups with this question: "What does it mean if your CEO comes to you and tells you to conduct a return-on-investment study to justify your company's training budget?" The answer is that you should start looking for a new job because the CEO has already decided to cut your training budget, outsource the training function, or eliminate it altogether. If you have done nothing to that point to demonstrate how training directly supports the achievement of the company's business goals, you will not be able to demonstrate the value of your training programs *post facto*.

In my 1997 book, *The Knowledge-Enabled Organization*, I asserted that fully half of the money spent on organizational training was wasted because what was learned in the classroom, or by other means, was never applied to the job. I see no reason to change that assertion today. What is needed is a new approach to organizational learning, one that ties all learning initiatives directly to company, business unit, team, and individual business goals and ensures that what is learned is actually applied to the learners' work to positively impact results – an approach that ensures that all training efforts are on target, where that target is business results.

Too Many Excuses

Over 40 years of working in organizational training, I have heard too many excuses by training professionals at all levels and in companies of many different sizes in many different industries for why they are not more involved in their companies' business processes. From my point of view, these are all lame rationalizations.

- Example #1: Several years ago, I attended a presentation by Tony Bingham, CEO of the Association for Talent Development (ATD) to a local chapter of that organization. He started his presentation with the same question that I used to start this chapter and offered the same answer to the question. At that presentation, I was seated at a table with several senior training directors from well-known financial institutions. One remarked, "How am I supposed to do that? I don't understand banking! I have a degree in instructional design, not an MBA!" and the others agreed with him.

- Example #2: I was hired by the head of a training group in a large systems consulting firm. This group of 25 professionals was responsible for the training of several thousand consultants in three divisions of the firm. The group had spent 18 months creating a planning document for line managers to plan for the training of their staffs. After agreeing to the assignment to review that plan, I asked him to send me, along with the planning document, a copy of the company's last three annual reports and a list of the top five business goals for each of the three business units they supported. The training director told me: "I really don't have access to that kind of stuff."
- Example #3: I met with the new training director of a technology company, a woman who had many years of experience in the industry. While she completed a conference call, I looked around her office. On the wall was a framed letter from the company's CEO welcoming her to the company. When she had completed the call, I

asked her about the letter. "I had it framed," she told me, "because I know it is the only time I will ever have any contact with the CEO."

- When I was first appointed to lead all networks-related training at DEC, I looked at a customer seminar on local area networks that was being offered by DEC's educational services organization. At the time, there were two competing technologies being used to build local area networks. DEC was the leader in Ethernet-based networks, while IBM (DEC's major competitor) was pushing token-ring networking. Educational Services had hired an outside consultant to give this seminar and he was advocating IBM's approach over DEC's. When I pointed this out to the management of the educational services organization, his response was: "It's a great seminar, and we're making a lot of money on it." Never mind that he was pushing business away from the company!

My question to these people, and to many others with whom I have worked and consulted, is "If you don't understand the business, how can you support it?" The most common reply I get is "We'd like to better understand the business, but we can't even get a meeting with the CEO, never mind getting a seat at the table. What can we do?"

The View from the Top

At the same time, surveys of CEOs continue to show that one of the key issues that keep CEOs up at night is the ability of the company to hire, train, and retain key employees to make the changes that will be needed to adapt to economic conditions over time and to achieve current and future business goals. When these executives look at their companies' training groups, they see little added value.

- "Where's our next generation of leaders going to come from?"
- "I sent one bright young guy to a very expensive external leadership program and nothing changed!"
- "We want to expand our product line and our geographic reach, but our employees don't have the needed skills!"
- "I am sick to death of the amount of money we are spending on external consultants. Why can't we develop these skills within the company?"
- "The consultants came up with a great plan, but we don't have the talent to implement the plan!"

The Default Approach for Training Groups

So, what do these training directors and their groups do? For most training groups, there are two approaches to their work:

- Approach #1: They respond to specific requests for training from various groups within the organization. With this approach, the training group waits until some business unit or functional group comes to them with a request. For example, the company is introducing a new system or technology and needs to get people trained to use it -- a new human resources system, a new manufacturing system, a new inventory system -- or it could be a new product line for which the salesforce needs training.
- Approach #2: They offer individual skills courses out of a catalog – the types of training that many companies offer their employees, e.g., new hire orientation, training for newly-appointed managers, training for new sales representatives, public speaking skills, etc.

Both of these approaches add value to their companies, for the training offered is certainly needed to keep the company going, but it never gets the training group involved in helping the company achieve its main business goals, never gets the training group involved in key strategic initiatives, never enables the training group to have a major impact on the company's business results.

When business leaders look at these training groups, they ask what real contribution they make and why it is costing so much money. They ask the groups' directors to do ROI studies to justify the decisions they have already made to reduce the training budget or to outsource or eliminate the training group.

The Key to Success: Critical Thinking

When I look back on my career in the training world and think about what has made me successful, the one skill that always comes out on top is critical thinking. Perhaps this is because my education was not in instructional design (although I have learned a lot about it throughout my career). My educational background includes a bachelor's degree in political sciences ("Politics is the art of the possible"), a master's degree in public administration, and a doctorate in the economics of education. When a favorite professor was retiring several years ago, I thought back on a seminar I took with him on "Cases and Problems in Economics and Finance" and realized that the critical thinking skills he had taught me were probably the most valuable part of my education in terms of my career in the training field. Critical thinking involves an awareness of assumptions and biases, of emotions, of strategy, and of trends. It requires you to question the *status quo*, to seek answers beyond "We've always done it that way," to look for root causes of problems.

Throughout my career, I have been known as an innovator and a disruptor. While many of my "innovations" seemed logical and easy to me, others often marveled at how easily I solved problems or came up with an effective approach that had never been tried before in the company. I have also been known as a "disruptor" and I have many times been disdained for disturbing the *status quo* with which people have been very comfortable ("We've been doing things this way for 20 years and have been very successful – and you're not going to change our minds").

Many of the stories I will tell in this book may seem obvious, but I have found that many solutions to problems that I found obvious were not as obvious to others. My hope is that while you may view some of my solutions as "obvious" you will find others of value. Here is one example from early in my training career.

My first job in training and development was as a curriculum manager at Digital Equipment Corporation[1] (DEC). My job was to plan for the training of field software support specialists on DEC's networks products -- I needed to keep track of new and revised products, plan what training was needed for each of them (ranging from a simple technical bulletin to a new course), and then contract with an internal development group to produce the

---

[1] An historical note: Digital Equipment Corporation was a pioneer in the development of mini-computers. At its height, around 1987, it employed 125,000 people around the world. The company was later bought by Compaq, which was subsequently bought by Hewlett-Packard.

needed training. When I started the job, I was told that I needed to get to know the people in product engineering, support engineering, product management, product marketing, and the technical support groups, and they would inform me of what new and revised products were in the pipeline.

Once I got to know all of these people, I found that 40 to 50% of my time was being spent on phone calls and emails from them and from the people in the field who needed the training to answer questions such as:

- When is this new product coming out?
- What training are you planning for this new product?
- When will the training be ready?

My question to my manager was "Is this the best use of my time?" His answer was "That's the way the system works. Get used to it."

My solution to the situation was to talk with the heads of the various groups with which I was working. I discovered that a lot of their time was being used answering the same or similar questions. To remedy the situation, I started quarterly meetings with the heads of the various groups where we produced a calendar of all new and revised products that were in the pipeline for the next six months and what training was going to be needed for each one. I then added my training plans to the calendar. Once we published this calendar of events to the various audiences, all of the queries we all handled on a daily basis declined by 75 percent.

To me, the answer was obvious. To many others, who had never questioned the longstanding work methods, it was a terrific innovation and was quickly adopted by the curriculum managers for the other product groups.

A Note on Critical Thinking

Given that I am advocating that you engage in critical thinking, which means that you should examine assumptions, biases, etc., it is only fair that I make clear two of my own biases.
- E-learning – I do not have an extensive background in e-learning. While I had established a virtual university at one company, where we provided e-learning programs to help thousands of people achieve a variety of technical certifications, I do not have a lot of experience in developing e-learning programs, and I am not up-to-date on the latest and greatest e-learning tools.
- Instructor-led training – While I acknowledge that e-learning has a lot to offer for training on certain types of skills, I do have a bias in favor

of instructor-led training. I will explain this in greater detail in Chapter 3.

A New Approach: The Learning Contract

Over the past 20+ years, I have given dozens of presentations to executive, human resources, and training groups on the topic of "The Fallacy of ROI Calculations," in which I argue against using return-on-investment (ROI) as a measure of training effectiveness. (I will include those arguments in Chapter 5 on Evaluating Learning Initiatives.) In that presentation, I have offered an alternative to traditional methods of planning and measuring training that I call a "Learning Contract." For many years, these audiences have asked when I would develop a toolkit for implementing this concept. This book is the answer to those requests.

Here is the basic format of the Learning Contract. Each element of it will be explained, with examples, in the following chapters. For each of the basic questions, I will offer a range of ideas for how today's training group can get answers. In most cases, this will require the training group to stretch beyond its traditional roles, to become more than trainers, to become *learning facilitators*.

- **Part I: Determining the Learning Need** -- The outcome of Part I is a learning agenda – What do people need to learn in order to meet their individual, group, and organizational goals?

- o What are the organization's goals?
  - o How do those goals cascade to the level of the business unit, team, and individual?
  - o What needs to change in order to meet those goals?
  - o What needs to be learned in order to make the needed changes?
- **Part II: Developing the Learning Plan** -- The outcome of Part II is a learning plan – How will employees learn what they need to learn as detailed in the Part I's learning agenda?
  - o What needs to be learned, when, and by whom?
  - o What learning methods will you use?
  - o Who will develop any needed learning materials?
  - o Who will deliver any needed training?
  - o How will you ensure that the needed learning takes place?
  - o How will learning be reinforced after any learning event?
- **Part III: Applying Learning to the Job** -- The outcome of Part III is an implementation plan – How will employees apply what they have learned in order to meet the set goals?
  - o How will the employee apply the learning to the job?
  - o What reinforcement or assistance will be available to help in this application?

- What changes in organizational, team, and individual performance are expected to result from the learning?

It is my experience that traditional training groups generally do a poor job of determining the learning need (Part I), a fair job of developing the learning plan (Part II), and almost always fail to ensure that learning is applied to the job (Part III).

My approaches to each of the above questions will be provided in the next chapters of this book. My hope is that you will get some new ideas from the discussions, examples, and suggestions so that your learning initiatives in the future can be "on target."

Chapter 2

The Learning Contract Part I: Determining the Learning Need

Part I of the Learning Contract is "Determining the Learning Need." It consists of four questions:
- What are the organization's goals?
- How do those goals cascade to the level of the business unit, team, and individual?
- What needs to change in order to meet those goals?
- What needs to be learned in order to make the needed changes?

The outcome from Part I is a learning agenda. It is the primary part of the Learning Contract where most training organizations fail. We'll examine each of the four questions and suggest ways for your training group to get the answers they need for each.

Question 1: What are the Organization's Goals?

From my point of view, all training efforts should start with an understanding of the organization's goals. Too often have I heard training directors make the types of excuses mentioned in Chapter 1:
- "I don't have an MBA (or an engineering degree or any other technical training related to the company's core business). How am I supposed to understand the company's business?"
- "I don't have a seat at the executive table, so I am totally out of the loop in terms of setting the company's goals or understanding the challenges facing the company."

While many training directors complain about not having a seat at the table, they do little to earn such a seat. CEOs complain that their training groups don't understand the company's business, but is it the CEO's job to make this happen? I would argue that it is the job of the training group to learn about the company's business and to demonstrate how the training group can add value to the company's efforts to meet its goals. Only by doing this can the training group earn its seat at the table. In too many cases, I have seen CEOs get so frustrated with the training group that they appoint a business leader (rather than a training professional) to head up the training function or the corporate university.

Not having a technical background related to the company's core businesses is NOT an excuse for not understanding the company's goals. Here are some ideas for how you can start learning about your company's business. While many of these ideas may seem obvious, I have found that few training directors take the time to implement them.

Idea 1: Gather Information About Your Company

There is a lot of information about your company available and easily accessible to you. In Chapter 1, I told the story of the head of a large training group for a major consulting firm who asked me to review a planning document. When I asked him for copies of the last few company annual reports and a list of the top goals for the business units his group supported, he told me that "I don't really have access to that type of information." I challenged him by asking him "If you don't understand the business goals, how can you support them?" He responded, "I used to work in those business units, so I know what they need." I then asked him how long he had been in the training group and he told me he had headed up the group for the past seven years. I asked, "Has the company's business changed much in those seven years?" He said that it had changed tremendously during that time. From my point of view, there was no excuse for his not keeping up with the company's goals.

Here are some ways that you can avoid this type of situation.

- *Spend time on your company's website.* You might be surprised how much information there is on the website to help you understand the company's goals. Read the press releases to learn about new developments. Read the biographies of the company's officers – you might find that some of the executives graduated from the same college as you, or that they have common hobbies or interests – this type of information can help you open doors and conversations with them.
- *Read the company's annual report.* The annual report not only contains financial statements, but also reviews major achievements and plans for the future. Annual reports can often be found on the company's website. If not there, ask someone in the investor services department for a copy.
- *Read reviews of your company's products or services.* Reading these types of reviews can give you insights into the company's customer base, how customers are using the company's

products and services and where they feel there is room for improvement.
- *Set up a search for news about the company.* This type of search (a free service) will send you a bulletin whenever the company is mentioned in the news or on the web and can provide great insights about how the company is doing and what it is planning.
- *Follow the company on Twitter and other services.* This will provide you with a variety of announcements and other news the company offers to the public. Listen to any podcasts that the company creates.
- *Follow the company on LinkedIn.* You will get any announcements from the company and from other employees of the company.

Idea 2: Talk with People in Different Business Units and Functions

Most people love to talk about their work. Find people to talk with in the various business units and functional areas in the company. Too often have I heard the excuse that "I tried to get an appointment to talk with the CEO (or the VP of a business unit) and couldn't get past the assistant." While it would be nice to get to know these people, they are busy and if they don't feel they have been getting value from the training group, it is unlikely they will feel it is a good use of their time to meet with you.

But you should realize that you don't need to go to the top of the organization to learn about it. Here are some ideas for how to start meeting with people to learn about the company and its work.

- *Have lunch in the company cafeteria with people you don't know.* Ask to sit down with people you don't know and ask them about their jobs? What do they do? How do they like their work? What training would they like to get to help them improve their work?
- *Use LinkedIn to identify people you could talk with.* Do a search of people in the company on LinkedIn and look for commonalities. Did they go to the same schools as you? Did you both work for the same company is the past? Do you follow the same sports teams or have other interests in common? When you find commonalities, connect with them, not just on LinkedIn, but also by calling or emailing them to ask to have lunch or to meet, and ask them about their work.
- *Participate in company-sponsored events.* Does the company sponsor softball or bowling teams? Is there a company-sponsored picnic or holiday party? Does it sponsor volunteer service in the community? These are all ways that you can get to know people from various functions and business units.

- *Talk with people who attend your training programs.* Even if you aren't teaching a particular program, ask the instructor if you can join the group for lunch and sit with people from the various groups who are attending the training. Ask your instructors if there are people in their classes who have a genuine interest in training/learning who you should get to know.

As you start networking within the company, ask each person to suggest other people who you should get to know. This doesn't take a great deal of time or effort – start by making one or two contacts each week and you'll be surprised at how quickly your network will grow and how much you can learn from these informal conversations. Build your network, and you will get a good start on understanding the company's business and the challenges people are facing in their jobs.

In one company where I worked, I had met the CEO, but had no real contact with him. He wasn't really interested in what my training group did. My conversations with a variety of people in the company led me to understand some issues that the CEO was struggling with in terms of the long-range plans for the company. I remembered a couple of articles I had read in the *Harvard Business Review* about the topic. I made copies of the articles and sent them to the CEO with a cover note. I never heard anything back from him.

Several months later, I ran across a book by the author of one of the articles, bought a copy, and sent it to the CEO with a cover note. A few days later, I got a call from the CEO asking me to get copies of the book for all the members of his executive committee and then to schedule time to lead a discussion of the topic with the committee. It was a great discussion and it greatly enhanced the credibility of the training group so that I could go to the CEO and his direct reports directly with regard to future projects.

Idea 3: Invite Speakers to Your Staff Meetings

As a training director, it is important for you to network and to better understand the company's business. It is just as important for your training staff to develop similar knowledge. When, through my networking activities, as described above, I have found someone who is knowledgeable about their segment of the company's business and who has a genuine interest in training and learning, I have often invited that person to come to one of my training group's staff meetings.

Ask the person to spend ten to fifteen minutes talking about their part of the business, the challenges they are facing, and how the training group might be of assistance. These can be very rich discussions. The more you know about the different areas of the business, the more intelligence you can gather, the better chance that you can get the attention of senior management.

When you do get someone from the business side to come to your meeting, make certain that you are also adding value to that person. First, make certain that you are keeping to your schedule – that you are not making the person sit through other parts of your meeting – make the person the focus of the meeting and then let him/her go. Follow up with a thank you note. Give them a book or some other favor (such as a notebook, a baseball cap, or some other item that you give to people who attend your programs). Later, if you run across an article or website that you think might interest that person, send a copy or a link with a note explaining why you think it might be of interest.

Idea 4: Assign Liaisons to Business Units and Functional Groups

If your training staff is large enough, consider assigning each member as a liaison to various business lines and to corporate groups, such as marketing, information technology, finance, etc. In a large company, it will be impossible for the training director to get to know all of these groups and keep up with developments within each of them in a timely manner. Try assigning each member of the training group to one business line or corporate function and make it part of their jobs to use all of the methods we are discussing here to learn about the assigned group, network with people from that group, and report on relevant developments at the regular meetings of the training group. If all goes well, the person may be able to get an invitation to sit in on the planning meetings of the group to which they have been assigned. They can also identify people to invite to speak to the entire training group (see Idea 3, above).

Idea 5: Create a Training Advisory Board

The training director for a large manufacturing company told me about her organization's training advisory board: "It's pretty worthless. When I started in this position two years ago, my manager, the vice president of human resources, recruited the ten business unit vice presidents to serve on the advisory board. The first couple of meetings were pretty good, but today we're lucky if five of them show up for any given meeting. We haven't seen several of them for more than a year."

"Can you tell me something about the meetings?" I asked.

"We meet on the first Monday morning of each month. We're supposed to start at 9:30. This gives the members a chance to get in early to check on important messages and such before coming to the meeting. By the time we have everyone here -- everyone who is coming, that is -- it is usually a little after 10. The afternoon subcommittee meetings are a joke. Half the time, one subcommittee or another has nobody there, and another will have only one person. For all practical purposes, the subcommittees no longer exist."

"What happens at a typical Monday morning meeting?"

"We start off by presenting the statistics for the past month: student hours, ratings, budget data, and so on. Then we talk about any new programs that have rolled out in the past month and any new ones scheduled for the next month."

"Is there any discussion?"

"Once in a while, someone will ask a good question about a new program. Most times, the questions focus on trends in enrollment. They also pay a lot of attention to the budget data -- how much we are spending and why. Once in a while, someone will pass along a comment about a particular program from one of their employees."

This company's advisory board (AB) was basically useless. I didn't blame the no-shows, and I wondered why the others bothered to come. But it doesn't have to be this way. The AB can be a vital strategic tool for any training director, whether managing a one-person shop or a company-wide function with dozens of employees.

Why Have a Training Advisory Board?

If training is to play a key role in helping the company and its employees succeed, it must endeavor to fully understand the company's business -- strategic business directions, core competencies, competitive challenges, new strategic business initiatives, etc. Whether the training group has one or dozens of employees, it is difficult to keep up with everything that is happening in the company, to understand all aspects of the company's various businesses, to understand all the competitive issues and pressures. A properly selected AB can provide key insights and understanding for the training group

At the same time, the AB's members can act as key advocates for training activities throughout the company. AB members can become sponsors and champions of key training initiatives and can provide pointers to key knowledge resources inside and outside the company. The AB can provide key linkages throughout the company, helping to ensure that the company's training resources are being utilized to maximum advantage.

Recruiting Members for your Advisory Board

Who should sit on your company's Advisory Board? In the earlier example, the AB had a very high-level membership -- the vice presidents/general managers from the company's ten major business units. Membership in some ABs tends to be focused more on functional lines -- representatives from sales, marketing, engineering, manufacturing, etc. In other companies, there is a mix of functional and business unit representation. Some companies recruit AB members, others call for volunteers.

Too often, business leaders consider it merely a matter of corporate citizenship to have a representative on the AB. "Sure, a training advisory board is a good idea, and I'll appoint someone from my group to be on it." After making this "commitment," the leader asks his staff, "OK, who has some time available to sit on this board?" without really considering (or caring) who the best representative would be.

In several cases where I have been asked to do a training session for a corporate training advisory board, it became obvious that many of the people in the room were there because their managers had told them to be there, and not because of any great interest in the work of the advisory board, or even in the general topic of training and development. An AB with the wrong membership is, at best, not useful and, at worst, a detriment to the achievement of the training group's goals.

To be an effective member of the AB, a person should have at least the following qualifications:

- A thorough understanding of the business unit or function he/she represents. The AB member should know how his/her function or business operates, what its key challenges and core competencies are, and be involved in the planning and execution of the function's or unit's strategic business initiatives. This is the key value that members can bring to the AB: the ability to help the training group understand the company's business.
- Credibility in his/her own organization. The AB member should be a person whose opinion carries weight in the organization -- "If Mary thinks this new program is a good idea, we should give it a chance."
- Time and willingness to help, to work with other AB members and with the training staff to fully understand the challenges being faced, and to work cooperatively to develop solutions to those challenges.
- A basic understanding of and belief in the value of knowledge and skills in meeting company,

organizational, and individual goals. Too often, ABs count within their membership a number of cynics who don't believe that the training group can do anything to help the company succeed. Without a reasonable attitude going in, AB members will not be effective and may end up being dysfunctional.

Some training directors feel that the higher the level of AB members, the greater the prestige of the training group within the company. They pressure their own vice president to recruit his/her peers to serve on the AB. While an AB composed of vice presidents can be effective, I believe it more important to ensure that AB members meet the above-stated criteria. Too often, as in the example above, vice presidents are too wrapped up in running their own businesses to have enough time or energy to devote to the AB.

It is also important that the training manager personally recruit AB members. The personal relationships between the training manager and AB members are of critical importance. If the training manager leaves selection and recruitment of members to his/her vice president, he/she is missing an important opportunity to start building these relationships.

When you have recruited your AB based on these qualifications, you have made a good start. But now that you have an AB, what do you do with it?

Advisory Board Orientation and Training

You have recruited your AB to help the training group better understand the company's business. And just as you have been so busy running your training group to develop this understanding yourself, so AB members have been so immersed in running their own businesses that they typically have not had time to develop a full understanding of your training business. Therefore, it behooves you, at the initial meeting of the AB, to provide some orientation to the training function, including:
- The charter and goals of the training group
- An overview of current and planned training programs and services
- Current statistics on participation, quality ratings, etc.
- Key internal and external relationships
- Key players from the training staff
- A tour of training facilities

If training in your company has not historically been viewed as a key contributor to the company's success, it may also prove useful to provide the AB with an overview of some success stories from other companies which demonstrate how an effective training function can add value to the company's strategic business initiatives.

Once the overview is complete, it is time to move on to defining the mission and role of the AB itself.

- Why have you asked these people to serve on the AB?
- How can training help them and the functions/organizations they represent?
- How can they help the training group?

How should the AB function at meetings and between meetings? It is a good idea to present some ideas for these ground rules, rather than to just throw out the question, sit back, and watch the action. While the first meeting should be run by the training manager, the AB should elect its own officers and give them responsibility for setting future agendas, of course with the assistance and advice of the training manager.

Members of the AB will be very familiar with the tools and methods they use to plan their own businesses but may not be at all familiar with those used by the training group. It will serve you well to familiarize AB members with your methodology, but in doing so, it is vital that you present your methods in a way they understand. Too often, we get so caught up in our own jargon, which makes perfect sense to us, that we fail to recognize that it may be totally incomprehensible to others who do not share our training and experience. For example, if you talk with a group of engineers about a "behavioral objective," they may laugh.

For example, in Chapter 1, I mentioned that one company's training director asked me to review a "Human Resources Development Planning Guide" which his group was just completing for use by his company's business unit managers. The guide presented a very comprehensive, systematic planning process which would enable a business manager to start with his/her business goals and work through a series of steps to determine the training and development activities required to enable employees to meet those goals. While the guide was very well done, it had two basic problems I felt would doom it to collect dust on the business managers' bookshelves: First, it was written in the language of training. As a training professional, the language made sense. For a business manager, it was all but incomprehensible. Second, the planning process detailed in the guide had no relationship to the company's well-established business planning processes. If I were a business manager reading the guide, my reaction would be: "I've just finished months of work developing my organization's plans using the company guidelines, and now you're telling me I have to start over from scratch just to determine training needs? You're crazy!" I should note that when I gave this feedback to the training director, he said that his group had spent 18 months developing the document and they weren't going to change it. When I checked back with him six months later, I found that my prediction had been accurate – business managers weren't using the document at all.

One of the first and most vital tasks you can undertake with your AB is to develop your own understanding of the company's business planning processes and then work with the AB to extend those processes to determine the learning needed to enable and facilitate the achievement of company, organizational, and individual goals. When the AB realizes that training is not trying to reinvent the wheel, but is trying to add value to the business (their business), the AB will become a powerful strategic tool for helping the training group achieve its own goals.

At this initial orientation and training meeting for the AB, it is also wise to identify a high priority company need on which you can focus your initial efforts. For example, is one division trying to implement TQM, introduce a new product line, improve customer service ratings, or move to concurrent engineering? Use the AB to help select one high priority area that you can work on together to test the planning methodology and, at the same time, provide evidence that training can really add value to the company's strategic business initiatives. A quick, effective response to this type of need will go a long way to establishing (or re-establishing) the credibility of your training organization within the company.

Running the Advisory Board

The AB should be convened on a regular, typically quarterly basis. Depending on the urgency of the items on the agenda, the AB may at times need to meet as frequently as once a month. But you must remember that this is an advisory board, not a management group. In the earlier example, it was ludicrous to think that the ten senior business unit managers in the company would take a full day each month to devote to the AB (and the first Monday of the month at that!).

This does not mean that the work of the AB takes place only four times a year. If the AB is convinced that it can add value to the company through its work, it will appoint its own subcommittees and work on key issues on a regular basis, outside the quarterly meetings. The training director should also provide AB members with regular monthly updates on key issues and programs and should feel free to call on AB members for advice or assistance as needed. At the same time, AB members should be calling the training director for assistance in program planning, to advise the director on changes in priorities or on upcoming strategic programs to which training can add value, etc.

Each quarterly meeting should be well-planned by the AB chairperson and the training director to ensure that the meeting time is well utilized and that AB members feel that their time at the meetings is worthwhile. The typical agenda items of reviewing enrollment statistics, budgets, and quality data should be handled in written reports delivered to AB members before the meetings -- little value is added to the training function or to the AB members by sitting and looking at tables of statistics and listening to someone reading them off the charts.

A properly constituted, properly run advisory board can be a key strategic tool for training directors who are seeking to make their organizations a key contributor to their companies' success. The AB can also help to revitalize a training group that has lost its focus and the AB members can become key advocates for the work of the group.

Question 1 – Summary

It is incumbent on the training group to develop an understanding of the company's business, its major goals, and its strategic initiatives. Only by doing so will you be able to establish the training group's credibility with business leaders and design learning initiatives that contribute to the company's success.

Question 2: How Do Those Goals Cascade to the Level of the Business Unit, Team, and Individual?

Understanding your company's goals and strategies a necessary beginning, but it is only a beginning. Those goals point you in the right direction. But in order to accomplish those goals, there have to be plans. How is the company planning to meet those goals? New products? Better marketing? Improvement in manufacturing processes? Or, more likely, a combination of plans and strategies that encompass many parts of the company's operations.

The next question in the Learning Contract is: How do those (organizational) goals cascade to the level of the business unit, team, and individual? It is vital for each business unit and each corporate function to understand its role in achieving the company's goals and then set its own goals to support the overall effort. If you don't understand the larger goals of your group, your business unit, and the company as a whole, how can you work toward their achievement?

Please note that the cascading of goals is NOT the responsibility of the training group. Every business unit, functional area, work team, etc., must work this out for themselves – what do each of them have to do to enable the overall company to reach its goals. But while your training group is not responsible for doing this, you must take responsibility for understanding the goals of each group within the company that you serve.

Here are a couple of examples of why this is important and how it can benefit the company.

- In one company, I worked on a training project for the credit and collections department. Credit and Collections is generally viewed as a low-prestige, relatively undesirable occupation – people there have to call customers to remind them that they must pay their bills, and sometimes have to tell sales reps that their customer isn't credit-worthy and has to pay cash if they want to buy the company's goods and services. People in credit and collections frequently dislike their jobs and the profession has a very high turnover rate. But this company's credit and collections group was different – they had very little turnover and people felt that they were making a great contribution to the company's success. As a result, this group outperformed the industry! Why was this group so successful? The manager of the group helped every employee understand how their work contributed to the larger company goals. She told them, "In our industry, the engineers may get most of the glory, and the sales reps may make the biggest salaries, but without our group's work, none of these people would get paid."

- In another industrial company, the maintenance department decided to apply for the Balridge Quality Award. This national program recognizes companies that have developed outstanding quality programs. When some executives questioned why a maintenance group felt it deserved this award, the head of the department replied, "We contribute greatly to the company's success. We keep our office facilities in such great shape that employees are happy to come to work each day, and customers who visit almost always tell the company how impressed they are with the design and cleanliness of our facilities. Additionally, we do such a great job in maintaining our factories that we haven't had an industrial accident in more than five years."

So how, as a training director or training group, are you going to learn about those plans as they cascade down the organization chart?

The methods for discovering these plans parallel those for discovering the company's goals, as explained earlier. Work with the network you have built among the various business units and corporate functions. Talk with people. And don't be upset if you find that there are big gaps in the plans – it happens.

I had been hired by a technology services company to build a "virtual university." The company had just signed partnership agreements with Microsoft and Cisco. Company leaders felt that these partnerships would be extremely beneficial to the company's future. As part of these agreements, the company pledged to train thousands of employees to help them achieve the technical certifications sponsored by those companies. My job was to establish a "virtual university" to help employees learn what they needed to pass the certification exams, primarily through on-line training.

I was able to accomplish this with the help of an excellent assistant director I had inherited and a small staff we had built to handle registrations and logistics. The company's problem was that while the senior organizational management set this arrangement, they had not convinced the heads of the various business units to build new services to utilize the newly-trained and certified employees. This wasn't a failure of training, it was a failure of company leadership: they had set the goals but had not developed the plans to use the new skill sets. As a result, many employees achieved their certifications and, when they found that there weren't opportunities to use their new skills within the company, left to seek employment where they could use them.

Here are some ideas for how you, as trainers, can get involved in the planning process.

Idea 6: Facilitate Planning Meetings

In most organizations, people constantly complain about the amount of time they waste in meetings, and rightly so because few people know how to properly plan and manage meetings. A great way for the training group to build credibility in the company is to help make meetings more productive.

- Does your training group teach a course on planning and managing meetings? Make a special effort at the start of the company's planning cycle to offer some workshops on planning and managing effective meetings. Not only will you be helping the company accomplish its planning more effectively, but you will be building credibility for the training group.
- If you don't teach a course on meeting facilitation, find a good article or book on the subject and send copies to the heads of the various business units and corporate functions ahead of the planning cycle with a note about how to use the materials and volunteer to answer any questions or consult with them on

developing the agenda for the planning meetings.
- How are your meeting facilitation skills? Volunteer the services of the training staff (assuming that they have the right skill set) to facilitate the planning meetings. I have facilitated dozens of planning meetings in companies that I worked for. Not only did having a neutral facilitator make the process more effective, it also built credibility for myself and my training group. And what better way to understand the plans than to facilitate the meetings where the plans are made?

Idea 7: Partner with Human Resources

Many, if not most, training groups report in to the company's human resources organization. If your training group cannot get into the planning meetings of the various business units and corporate functions, the odds are that the human resources staff will be participating in the planning efforts. If your human resources organization has business partners assigned to these groups, they should be an integral part of the planning team and, if they cannot get you a seat at the meeting, they should be able to provide you with information on the plans being made.

In one company, where I was the one-person training staff, I trained the human resources business partners (HRBPs) on meeting facilitation skills, and they then volunteered to facilitate the planning meetings for their assigned groups. Not only were the HRBPs thrilled to have this new skill set to demonstrate their value to the groups they supported, they were then able to provide me with the information I needed on the plans being made. This is even more important for answering Question 3, below.

Question 3: What Needs to Change in Order to Meet Those Goals?

Change is difficult. People are naturally resistant to change, especially if they are comfortable with the status quo. Change can also take many forms – changes in organization, changes in personnel, changes in equipment, changes in procedures, changes in systems, and so on. Many changes have no connection to the training group, so your focus must be on those changes that have a learning/training/knowledge component. Unfortunately, in most companies the focus of planning for change focuses primarily on changes that require major investments, e.g., do we need to re-tool a factory or introduce a new information system or create a new marketing campaign?

In the early 1980s, I was director of education and training for the Networks and Communications Marketing (NAC) group of Digital Equipment Corporation (DEC). At this time, a new technology, local area networking (LAN) was being introduced and DEC saw this as an opportunity to greatly expand its network products and services offerings. This was going to require major changes, including:

- Major changes in sales methods – network sales would require sales support personnel from both field service and software services to work closely with sales reps to develop customer proposals and to install and service the solutions once they were sold. Historically, these groups did not work together and we would have to break down their silos as well as develop new rewards systems.
- DEC had built its business selling mini-computers to technical personnel. The new LAN solutions would require us to work with business managers, a new audience with which our field personnel had little experience and with whom they felt discomfort. This would require a whole new approach to marketing and sales.
- The projected growth rate of the networks business would require the training of many more personnel than currently existed. New products were going to be introduced at a

rate that the company's existing training methods could not keep up with.

So, there were a lot of changes that needed to be made to meet the goals. My job was to determine how the training function could facilitate those changes. The result was the creation of a program that became known as Networks University. The Networks University program was unique, not just for DEC, but for the entire industry. Throughout this book, you will learn more about its unique features and methods. For now, here are some of the features that I included in the Network University programs:

- Both marketing and technical sessions on new products and services, including hands-on demonstrations.
- Team-building exercises to get employees from the different functions working together.
- Presentations by external consultants and business school professors to help employees understand the market challenges for the new technology.
- A boot camp to get new employees up to speed quickly so that they could benefit from the main agenda of Networks University.
- Involvement of everyone in the DEC Networks world – engineers, marketing personnel, strategic planners, business unit executives, etc. – to facilitate the two-way exchange of

information and ideas between the field personnel and the corporate functions.

Networks University was a week-long program held twice a year in the United States for an audience of 400 to 600 people, twice a year in Europe for an audience of 200-350 people, and once a year on the Pacific Rim for an audience of 150-200 people. In each six-month cycle, there were from 40 to 70 separate sessions ranging from an hour to three full days, and in each cycle, 80% of the content was new.

Change requires learning – you can't change without learning. Are you re-tooling a factory? Then you need to train people on the new equipment and work methods. Are you introducing a new corporate information system? People need to be trained on how to convert from the existing system to the new system and how to use the new system.

Are you trying to rapidly build a new networks and communications business? It requires learning – learning on everyone's part, from top executives to the field personnel who would be selling, installing, and servicing customer solutions.

Idea 8: Offer Resources on Leading, Managing, and Dealing with Change

Years ago, I attended a symposium at MIT on quality programs in manufacturing. One of the speakers was the CEO of a successful high-tech company in the Boston area. He spoke about a conversation that he had had with a Japanese professor who was working as a fellow at MIT.

"I have been trying to implement quality measures in our manufacturing processes, but the progress is very slow," the CEO said. "There's been a lot of resistance to the changes."

"How have you been involved in the quality program?" asked the fellow.

"I approved the budget for the quality office and sent an email to all company employees telling them of the new program and saying how important it was," replied the CEO.

"There is your problem," said the fellow. "If you want the quality effort to be successful, you must *live the change*. You must be personally involved in the change effort and make your involvement very visible to your employees."

Change itself requires learning – *how to lead a major change effort* for top company executives, *how to manage change* for those who will be implementing the changes, and *how to deal with change* for the rank and file employees whose jobs will be affected. In too many companies I have worked for, consulted to, and observed I have seen executives struggle for weeks or months to define needed changes. But once they have settled on what needed to change and announced those changes, they assumed that everything would go smoothly and that no one else in the company would suffer through the angst that they had just gone through.

It is not the job of the training group to define the changes that are needed. In fact, the planning of change is usually invisible to the training group. But even if it is invisible to you, this doesn't mean that you cannot be aware of it. You should have many sources within your network to learn about the change efforts:

- If you have built an advisory board, its members are the key resources who can advise you of upcoming changes and how the training group could help facilitate the change process.
- Even though the training group is not directly involved in the planning process, your human resources group should be. Talk with your human resources business partners about how you can help.
- If you have built your network within the company using the suggestions earlier in this chapter, you can talk with those people about what is happening.

Depending on the level of credibility your training group has in the company, and depending on how involved company leadership wants your group to be, there are several levels of effort that you can implement:

- At the top level, you could provide training for company executives on planning and leading change efforts. At this level, you might want to bring in an external consultant or professor to work with the highest levels of the company. At one company, I worked with the CEO to identify a local business school professor who not only advised the CEO but also facilitated the planning sessions of the executive committee.

  In many companies, arranging this type of assistance for the CEO and the executive committee would not be seen as a responsibility of the training director. In this case, I had heard of the need for assistance from my manager, the vice president of human resources, and suggested to her the idea of bringing in some outside help for the CEO. She liked the idea and got the approval of the CEO. I then identified several possible candidates and had each interview with the CEO so that he could choose the one with whom he was most comfortable. My role here was not as a trainer, but as a *learning facilitator*, as will be explained in Chapter 3.
- At the next level (senior managers), you could offer training on planning for and executing change. There are courses offered by universities and training companies on these topics and you could either get one of your trainers certified to teach a

course or bring in an outside trainer. If there isn't the necessary support for bringing in outside training, you could create a list of available external courses and provide it to your advisory board members and people in your internal network.
- For the rank and file employees who have to deal with the stress of change, there are any number of courses that you could make available, ranging from dealing with stress to being an effective team member.
- Even if your training group doesn't have the immediate resources (or credibility) to offer such courses, you can make learning resources available to employees at all levels. You could create a website for your training group where you can list available internal and external programs and a reading list of well-regarded books and articles on relevant topics.

Let me re-emphasize here that it is not the job of the training group to identify the changes that need to be made throughout the company in order to meet the stated goals. But it is your job to learn about the needed changes so that you can plan the training agenda to enable and facilitate those changes. At best, the training group will be viewed as a key resource for this purpose by company leaders. At worst, and too often, the focus of company leaders will be on investments in technology, development of new products and services, reorganizations, etc., and will not include training/learning as a major factor in the change efforts. This means that the training group, in order to demonstrate its value, will have to use its network to learn what changes are being planned and to determine where it can add the most value to the change efforts.

Let me go back to the origins of Network University. I had originally been recruited from another job at DEC to head up all networks-related training, both internal and external. While I was hired by the head of a new networks services group, I reported into DEC's Educational Services organization. Educational Services was a large organization (about 1500 employees) responsible for all internal and external training in the company as well as for technical documentation.

After building my network in the networks world and examining how Educational Services did networks training, I found that its longstanding methodology was not able to get the job done. When DEC's main business was mini-computers, with new models coming out every three-to-five years, development of training materials could take a year or more to produce. The group had a 4-inch binder that specified every step of its methodology, from how to write a question for a needs assessment to the font style to use in instructional materials.

After completing my own needs assessment, I went to the management of Educational Services with a list of changes that I felt were needed to meet the needs of the network business, was told "That's not how we do things," and given a copy of the methodology binder. When I presented my ideas on how we needed to do things (including the basic model for Networks University) to meet these needs, I was again told "That's not how we do things."

As a result, I went to the head of the new Networks marketing group and presented my plan to him. His response was "That's great! Go do it!" When I explained that Educational Services management would not allow me to do it, he picked up the phone, called the vice president of Educational Services, and hired me to implement my plan as part of the marketing group.

This got me a seat at the table, but it didn't fully establish my credibility with the group. At the first meeting I attended as part of the marketing group, I was challenged to identify and meet a critical short-term training need. DEC's main competitor was IBM. In the networks world, DEC's Digital Network Architecture (DNA) competed directly against IBM's Systems Networks Architecture (SNA). At the same time, DEC had a set of products that worked cooperatively with SNA. But the company had never offered its employees any training on SNA, so it was difficult to compete against SNA and equally difficult to sell products that cooperated with SNA. I had tried in vain to get Educational Services to provide training on SNA, but was told first that the company policy was never to offer training on competitors' products and, second, even if they allowed it to happen, I would have to come up with $100,000 to get one of their course developers trained on SNA so that they could develop the course and that it would take 12 to 18 months before any training was available.

I suggested to the networks marketing group that we really needed this training. When the relevant marketing manager and product manager agreed, I was given the assignment. I found an excellent (attested to by several networks employees who had attended) two-day SNA course from a training company and brought it in-house. I also worked with the marketing manager and the product manager to put together a third day of training on how to compete against SNA and on how to sell DEC's products that cooperated with SNA. Within 30 days, I had trained more than 100 DEC employees with this program and got rave reviews.

I also made another suggestion to the marketing group. The external instructor for this course was well known in the industry and did training on SNA more than 120 days a year around the world. When I first spoke with him, it was clear that he knew nothing about DEC's networks offerings. I suggested to the marketing manager that we pay him for an extra day of his time and use that time to educate him on DEC's approach to and products for networking. The marketing manager was thrilled to have this opportunity to get the word out to this expert.

This quick victory was what earned me the credibility to sit at the planning table.

Question 4: What Needs to be Learned in Order to Make the Needed Changes?

This is the final question in Part I of the Learning Contract. The answers to this question determine the company's learning agenda and set the goals for your training group. What we are talking about here is doing a needs assessment. We'll discuss this more in the next chapter, but here's an example of how I did needs assessments for DEC's Networks University.

As stated earlier, each semi-annual Networks University program included from 40 to 70 different sessions ranging from one hour to three full days. To select the topics to include in each program, I surveyed:
- Marketing managers and product managers to determine what new products and services were in the pipeline.
- The target audience, i.e., the people who attended the previous program – what did they

feel they needed to learn? What would add value to their jobs?
- The technical support groups in the networks world – what questions were they being asked regularly? What problems were they seeing that we could avoid if we provided training at the next program?
- The competitive analysis group – what were other companies that we were competing against doing and how could we prepare the audience to best that competition?
- We also examined the feedback sheets from the previous program to see what the participants found most valuable and least valuable.

The point here is that you need to make certain that what you are proposing and developing will meet the needs of your audience and that you are only offering training solutions where training, rather than other factors beyond the training group's control, is the right solution. One other point here. I had said that in each week of training, we offered 40 to 70 different sessions, ranging from an hour to three full days. Obviously, no one could attend every session. What we did was to let each participant decide which sessions to attend. While we did make suggestions on "tracks" that could be followed and we made all of the materials from every session available to every participant, we left it to the individual participant to decide which sessions were most relevant to their work.

But what happens if your company doesn't value training? What if the company's leaders don't view the training group as a valuable resource that can help the company achieve its goals? This happens much too often. Here is an example from my own experience.

At the company where I founded the virtual university to help employees achieve Microsoft and Cisco certifications, I was told that the company policy was NOT to invest anything in training. The only reason they had established the virtual university was because they wanted the partnerships with these two companies, and the commitment to helping employees achieve these certifications was a requirement imposed by Microsoft and Cisco.

Once my training group had the virtual university up and running smoothly, and the training staff was handling the daily operations efficiently, I met with my boss and two human resources vice presidents to whom I reported. I asked them what the next challenge was. Did the company want to offer management and leadership training? Was there a need for sales training? What other training needs could we satisfy and use to add value to the company's operations?

I was told that my total job was what we already had set up. The company had no interest or plans to invest in any training beyond what we had already established. In fact, after this meeting, my boss came into my office, closed the door, and asked me: "Do you know how much damage you just did to yourself by even suggesting that the company invest anything in additional training?"

That comment certainly depressed me. Once the virtual university was up and running, and my training staff was doing a great job running things, what was there for me to do? I knew there had to be additional learning needs and that there were certainly ways in which we could provide additional value to the company, but I certainly wasn't going to get any support from my boss or the human resources organization.

So, I started networking with people in the various business units. From these conversations, I learned that the business unit leaders felt a great need to do a better job at managing projects. An employee in the company's Belgian operations had developed a set of tools and reporting formats that the company wanted to adopt worldwide, but there was no current way to train people on their use. Further, some of the large customer projects on which we were bidding required that the project leaders have certification as a Project Management Professional (PMP), a certification from the Project Management Institute, and the company only had a couple of people with that certification.

Once I learned of this need, I kept talking with people from the various business units and different

geographic locations throughout the company to determine the size of the need. What I found was:
- The business unit leaders wanted to provide a basic awareness of project management and what went into it for 400 to 500 people throughout the company.
- There were 100 to 150 people who were current project managers who needed training on project management and control to better do their jobs and who also needed to start using the project management methods and formats from the Belgian operations.
- There were 20 to 30 people who needed to achieve the Project Management Professional (PMP) certification.

How could the training group meet these needs? I had no expertise and very little background in project management, so I started doing research.
- I spoke with the person in Belgium who had developed the project management materials that the company wanted to use across the globe.
- I spoke with the two PMPs within the company to learn more about the certification and how they achieved it.
- I spoke with people at the Project Management Institute about the certification and the requirements to achieve it.

- I spoke with people at several universities and training vendors that offered programs on project management.
- I searched for resources on the internet.

Once I had done my research, I devised a plan. I knew that the plan had to entail as little expense to the company as possible – I had already been told by my boss that the company had no interest in investing in any type of training. The plan also had to require a minimum of time off the job – the powers that be had explicitly told me time spent in formal training a "waste of company resources." The challenge was that most of the project management programs I found required attendance at eight to twelve classroom courses, at a tuition cost of $15,000 to $25,000, and a time commitment to attend classes of between 25 and 40 days. This clearly was not going to be acceptable to the company.

My plan had three components:
- For the several hundred people who needed awareness of project management, I found a book and a CD that provided an introduction to the subject. The cost of the book and CD was about $40, and I planned to get 20 copies of each and create a lending library for them.
- I worked with a local university to customize a five-day program they offered on project management and control. The two

customizations were first, the inclusion of a case study for the types of projects my company did and, second, the inclusion of instruction on the materials from our Belgian operation. The cost of this program, for the 100 to 150 people who needed it, came out to about $750 per person.
- I found a vendor that offered a series of three eight-week distance learning courses to prepare students for the PMP examination. These courses were more academic in nature because that was what was required for the PMP exam. When I reviewed the outlines of the three courses with the instructor of the five-day project management and control workshop, he said that that workshop covered everything in the first of the three courses. I arranged with the distance learning provider to have the first group of students who took the workshop to take an exemption exam for that first distance learning course and, when everyone passed the exam, they exempted everyone completing the workshop from taking that course, so there were only two eight-week distance learning courses required. These courses cost $800 per person per course, or $1600 in total.

I drew up a formal proposal for this training and distributed it the heads of the business units and to my boss. My boss told me, "You're going to get hammered. I told you the company isn't going to spend any money on training."

A few days after distributing the proposal, I got a call from the company's vice president of business development. He wanted me to make a formal presentation of the proposal the following week. This vice president was responsible for the partnerships with Microsoft and Cisco and was a major power in the company. He also had a reputation for tearing down other people's ideas and leaving them with no self-esteem. When I told my boss about the command performance, he said I was going to be taught a hard lesson.

When the appointed time came for my presentation, I was surprised at the size and composition of the audience. All of the business unit heads were there, along with my boss and the two vice presidents of human resources and a variety of other people who, in an earlier time, would have attended events at the Roman Coliseum just to see the blood being shed.

I made my presentation, explaining the need I had discovered and the alternatives I had considered along with the reasons I had chosen the components I had included in the proposal. He had a number of questions that I answered – I was well prepared. Finally, the vice president said that it was a great plan and that he would provide me with a list of the people he wanted to be enrolled in the program first.

Before Proposing a Training Solution, Make Certain that Training Can Solve the Problem

Too often, a company executive will come to the training group asking the group to deliver training to his/her group, only later to discover that the problem the executive was trying to solve required a solution other than training. In many of these cases, the training group develops and delivers training according to the executive's request, only to find that the training had no effect on the problem. And the blame for the failure is assigned to the training.

I once met two trainers from a Fortune 100 company. Their specialty was team training. They had given a three-day workshop to teams throughout the company to help them improve their team performance. They told me of getting a request from one manager in the company to give the training to her team. When the class assembled for the first time, they asked the group what their primary team goals were -- and got no answers. They asked what challenges the group faced as a team – and got no answers. Finally, they asked if the group members felt that they were a team. Then, they got answers. "We're not a team. She gives each of our own assignments and measures our work individually. She gets angry if she sees us trying to help each other, or even talk with each other. Not one of us feels like we are part of a team."

The trainers then did what I believe was the right thing to do (and something that I think most trainers would avoid doing): they sent the group back to their jobs and went to see the manager to explain about teamwork and team leadership. They invited her to a workshop on team leadership and told her that they would be happy to conduct the team workshop once she had decided to transform her group into a team.

The point here is that these trainers could have conducted their workshop, a workshop that had been very successful in helping many teams throughout the company, and it wouldn't have made a bit of difference.

Here is a second example from my own experience. A product manager came to see me one day. He said that his group had developed a great new set of products – they were industry-leading products that were getting great reviews from the industry press and the few customers who were using them. The problem, he said, was that the company's salesforce wasn't selling them. He asked me to develop a one-day sales training program on the products and to take the training to sales teams around the world. "Figure out how much money you'll need, and I'll make sure you get it – whatever it takes!"

Before putting together a proposal for him, I called a few sales reps and sales managers I knew from my network. I asked them if they knew about the new product set and what training they felt they needed on the products. The answers I received from them all were exactly the same: "These are great products. We know about them and don't need any training." So, I asked them why they weren't selling them. "They don't appear on our goal sheets. We get no credit towards our quotas or toward the annual sales awards for selling them. So, we focus on selling products that help us achieve our goals."

My training group could have taken the product manager's money and developed the best training program that ever existed. My training staff could have traveled all over the world delivering the training. And it wouldn't have made one bit of difference in the sales numbers.

I went back to the product manager, who was relatively new to the company, and explained that this wasn't a training problem and didn't require a training solution. "Then what can I do to get the products sold?" he asked. I suggested that he go to the sales management team and try to get the products included on the goal sheets for sales reps. "If you want to spend some money, try offering prizes for the sales reps who sell the most in a given period of time."

Often, someone will come to the training group with a specific request: "Can you provide training on Topic X for my group?" This is always a welcome request – you are the training group and responding to such a request demonstrates your value to the company. But, before accepting the assignment, you should ask one vital question: "What is the problem you are trying to solve?" Without understanding the problem, you can't deliver the right solution, even if the requestor thinks that he/she has already determined that the requested training is the solution.

I got a call from the training director for a state correctional system. She said that she had read an article I had written about learning organizations and wanted to know if I could deliver a half-day seminar on the "five disciplines" as described in Peter Senge's book, *The Fifth Discipline*. She wanted me to do the seminar twice, once for the commissioner of corrections and his staff and a second time for the 22 prison superintendents. I said that I could do that, but I also asked if we could first sit down to talk about it.

When we met, I asked her why she wanted to do this training. She told me that she was the co-chair of a task force whose job was to design a new "inmate management system" for the correctional system. She said that the commissioner had set aside $5 million for the new system and while he was enthusiastic about it and got support for the system in meetings, a number of his direct reports were nay-saying the project behind his back and that when her task force met with some of the superintendents, they were not supportive, so the task force was making little if any progress.

I asked her why she felt that doing this half-day seminar would help the situation. She said that she had just finished reading Senge's book and thought that if she could get all of the players to learn and use Senge's five disciplines, the job of the task force would be a lot easier. I told her that she was probably right. But I also told her that the half-day seminar she wanted probably wouldn't do the job. When she asked why I thought that, I asked her how long it had taken her to read Senge's book (a massive tome), and she said that she saw my point and asked what I would suggest to get her task force's work back on track.

"Let's talk with the commissioner and some of his staff and with a few of the superintendents," I suggested. Over the next week, we met with half a dozen people. What we heard was that the nay-sayers on the commissioner's staff recognized that the new system was going to be a major change and "the correctional system has never handled change well." From the superintendents we heard comments such as "We've tried to do this several times before over the past 15 or 20 years and it never happened, so why bother?"

The solution I provided was to do the two half-day seminars, but the topic was changed to "Leadership and Change." I spent an hour talking about the need for leadership in any change effort and told them that the new inmate management system represented a major change for the correctional system. I then asked each person why the new system was important to them and what benefits there would be to their work and to the correctional system from the new inmate management system. When someone couldn't provide an answer, I asked the deputy commissioner for administration (who would own the system and who had been one of the major nay-sayers behind the commissioner's back) to help the person out. "Why is the new system important to his or her work?"

By the end of the two sessions, everyone recognized the importance of the task force's work and had made a commitment to support the development of the new system. We then held a full-day planning session with the two groups together to plan the next steps for the task force.

The training director and the commissioner later told me that the intervention I did got the project back on track. The important point here is that if I had just fulfilled the original request, nothing would have changed, and the system would never have been implemented.

The moral here is that *before you propose a training solution, make certain that the problem you are trying to solve is one that can be solved by training.*

Use Your Critical Thinking Skills and Teach Others to Use Them as Well

After giving a presentation at a national conference, I was contacted by a marketing vice president from a well-known mutual fund company. He told me that he was planning a new curriculum for near-to-retirement employees from companies whose 401-K business was with his mutual fund company. Aside from the obvious fact that people need education to plan for their retirement, I asked him why the company was investing in this new initiative. He told me, "Obviously, we are trying to increase our business, and we feel that if we offer this type of education, we are more likely to win proposals for our services from more companies."

I then asked him if they had done any research on whether offering such education would make a difference in their sales results. "No," he said. "But it seems obvious to me." I then asked him to outline the processes that the company went through to win new clients for the 401-K business. Once this was done, we discussed how learning could help improve each step of the process, thereby improving the company's success rate for winning

new business. By questioning his assumptions, we came up with two other strategies to improve business results.
- First, the group that wrote proposals to win new business was overwhelmed with work. The company regularly received requests for proposals from two sources: their own sales reps who had established contact and held discussions with potential client companies and unsolicited proposals from many other companies. These other companies may or may not have been holding discussions with other mutual fund companies, but in doing due diligence to select a 401-K vendor had sent their requests for proposals to a wide range of providers. It turned out that the success rate for proposals to companies with which his sales reps had held discussions was over 50 percent; for companies with which his sales reps had had no contact, the success rate was under 10 percent. So, an effective strategy was to limit proposal development to those companies with which sales reps had held discussions. This allowed the proposal group to do a better job on those proposals and it eventually led to a 20 percent improvement in the success rate.
- The second conclusion from our discussions was that the 401-K administrator in client companies was either the decision maker or a key influencer in selecting the 401-K vendor.

His company had done nothing in terms of educating this audience, so we designed a curriculum specifically for this role.

The point here is that by using critical thinking, we were able to derive better solutions than if we had relied solely on his personal experience in the industry. By asking the right questions, we found additional ways to add value to his business goals.

Learning Contract Part I – Summary

The purpose of Part I of the Learning Contract is to determine what needs to be learned to enable and facilitate the achievement of organizational, group, and individual goals. Most training groups do very poorly at this task. As explained, it is incumbent on the training group to learn all it can about the company, its business(es), its goals, and its strategic initiatives, for only by developing such knowledge can the training group ensure that its efforts add real value to the company.

Chapter 3

The Learning Contract Part II: Developing the Learning Plan

Part II of the Learning Contract involves developing the learning plan. To do this, you must answer six questions:
- What needs to be learned, when, and by whom?
- What learning methods will you use?
- Who will develop the needed learning materials?
- Who will deliver the training?
- How will you ensure that the needed learning takes place?
- How will learning be reinforced after any learning event?

Of these six questions, most training groups focus on questions 1, 2, 3 and 4, above. We'll start with those questions. Here's a first example from my experience.

The New Inventory System

I got a call one day from the company's chief financial officer (CFO) asking me to meet with him. The meeting included several of his staff members, including the person who would be responsible for the administration of a new inventory management system and the person who would be the technical guru and primary troubleshooter for the system. The CFO said that the company had just invested $500,000 in a new capital goods inventory system to keep track of all the equipment the company had worldwide including office furniture, manufacturing equipment, computers, etc. The vendor for this system said that they could develop an e-learning program to train people to use the new system at a cost of $100,000. His question for me was whether it was worth the investment.

Related to Part II of the Learning Contract, I needed to determine the size of the audience, what they needed to learn, how quickly the training was needed, (all related to the first of the six questions) and what subject matter expertise was available (to help determine who would develop the needed training). Here are the questions I asked and the answers I received:

- Question: How many people needed to be trained? Answer: There would be about 500 people who had to enter data into the system and about 25 "super-users" (people who would provide local training, back-up support, and local trouble-shooting) around the globe.
- Question: How difficult was it to use the system? Answer: The system was actually very easy to use. The user needed to attach an identification tag to each piece of equipment and then enter the name, serial number, tag number, and location of each piece into the system. According to the people who had worked to design the system and who would administer it, the use of the system was almost intuitive.
- Question: Do we have the subject-matter experts available in-house or would we need to rely on the vendor for subject-matter expertise? Answer: We had the expertise in-house.
- Question: When do you need the training done? Answer: This was one of the CFO's major concerns. The vendor said it would take four to five months to develop the proposed e-learning program. The CFO said that he wanted to implement the system as soon as possible.

The training solution for this new system will be discussed later in this chapter. The point here is that you need to answer all of the questions in Part II to really understand the problem you are trying to solve *before* proposing a solution. We'll examine the six questions in Part II, one by one.

Question 1: What Needs to Be Learned, When, and By Whom?

From Part I of the Learning Contract, you should already understand the problem you are trying to solve. So, what do people need to learn? Before starting, make certain that learning is the right solution to the problem, as explained at the end of Chapter 2. Once this determination is made, you will need to rely on subject-matter experts to help you understand the content and translate that content into training materials. This expertise may come from people in your training group, other experts within your company, or external subject-matter experts.

Working with Subject-Matter Experts

Some examples of when your training group might need to work with subject-matter experts:
- There is a training need for a new product or service that your company is planning to introduce to the market. The training group may be asked to develop training for those who will sell the product, those who will install the product, those who will provide the service, etc.
- There is a training need for employees who will use a new company system, e.g., SAP, or Oracle,

or a new manufacturing system, a new call center response system, or a new performance management system.

Supporting the Introduction of a New Product or Service by your Company

In many companies, a member of the training staff may be assigned to develop new training materials or a new instructor-led or e-learning program, for a new product or service. If this is how your company works, you should try to become part of the product development and introduction team as early in the development process as possible, and certainly no later than the beginning of beta testing of the new product or service. The more you can learn, and the earlier you can learn it, the better off you are. Sometimes, the product development team will resist putting a training person on the team - "What do they know? How can they possibly help us? We're the engineers/product designers/service developers - we know what we need to do and putting that training person on our team is only going to slow us down." Try this argument to overcome these types of objections from the technical staff (SMEs):

- The product isn't going to do the company any good unless our salespeople know how to sell it, our service people know how to install it and fix it, and our customers know how to use it. We want to make certain that the training for all of these groups is ready when you are ready to announce the product. We don't want to hold up the product introduction because we can't provide the needed training to all of these groups in a timely manner.

In some cases, the product or service may be so complex that you really do need to have the SME provide the initial training. In these cases, the SME may object to working with someone from the training group with an argument such as: "Look. I know this product inside and out. I'll just get up and talk about it. The technical staff, from here in the company or from customers, will be so impressed with the depth of my knowledge and have such confidence in my technical knowledge and abilities, it won't make any difference whether we have pretty training materials or not - they'll get all the answers from me and they can take notes." Try these arguments to overcome these objections:

- This may be true for the customers who will participate in the beta-test for the product. But if the product takes off like you hope it will, you aren't going to be able to provide all the training yourself. And while customers for the beta-test may be satisfied with your notes, as more and

more customers buy the product, they are going to expect that the training materials are as professional as the product. We can help you put together a more professional presentation for your initial training session and, at the same time, learn what we need to learn about the product so we can start working on the formal customer training materials.
- We acknowledge your technical expertise. But we are the experts at training our internal support groups and our customers. Let us help you translate your technical jargon into language that your audience will understand. Let us help you put together a powerful, professional presentation - it can only make you look better.

I was in charge of a customer seminar/road show to introduce and demonstrate the company's newest products. The show was being professionally produced and we had recruited speakers from marketing and product management to present the seminar. Several of the engineers who would be traveling with the seminar to support the equipment and do demonstrations asked if they could also be speakers at the seminar. I had no objection to this, but I insisted that they take the same presentation skills workshop that all of the other speakers were required to take to prepare for the seminar. The engineers objected: "We don't need to waste our time on this training. Customers will see that we know what we are talking about and will soak up the information from us. Our technical expertise will be sufficient without wasting our time to learn how to present." I forced the issue and got them to take the workshop, despite their protests.

A few years later, I was visiting one of the company's sites and, at lunch time, one of the engineers who had participated in the seminar sat down next to me in the cafeteria. After exchanging greetings, he told me, "You know, I just got a big promotion." "Congratulations," I said. "I'm sure it was well-deserved." "You know," he continued, "I've been thinking about it, and I concluded that the presentation skills workshop you made me attend a few years ago was probably as much responsible for the promotion as my technical knowledge and skills." "That's an interesting observation," I replied. "Why do you say that?" "It's just that engineers in general are such poor presenters, the fact that I have good presentation skills separated me from my peers who are just a bright technically as I am but can't make a good presentation to save their lives."

Some Additional Strategies for Working with SMEs

Here is another strategy I have used to work with an SME when it was clear that the SME, rather than the training staff, needed to do the actual training. I once asked an engineer if he could put together a 2-hour training session as part of a larger training program I was developing. "Sure," he said. "Tell me when and where I need to be and I'll show up and do the session." I offered to have one of the instructional designers on my training staff work with him to organize the presentation and prepare materials for the training participants. "I don't have time for that," the engineer said. "Just tell me where I need to be, and I'll provide the training. Just make sure that I have at least one big white board that I can draw on." I knew that the engineer was very busy with other projects, but he was the best SME the company had on the topic. I wasn't going to win this argument. Instead, I asked, "Could you give the presentation twice? Once, say next week. The second time will be about a month from now when we hold the formal training session." He agreed. The next week, he did his two-hour presentation. I had put these people in the audience for this preliminary presentation:

- An instructional designer
- A graphics designer

- Two members of the target audience for the training
- A camera operator

The two members of the target audience helped to focus the presentation on the needs of those who would be trained. These two people made comments on what material was on target, what material was superfluous for the target audience, and what topics should be added to the presentation.

The instructional designer and the graphics designer who attended used their notes from the session, along with the video we recorded, to prepare an agenda for the later training session and to prepare slides (rather than the hand-drawn diagrams the SME had put on every inch of the white board) and other materials for the target audience. About a week before the main training session, I went to see the SME. I went through the agenda with him and gave him the slides and materials that my staff had prepared. "Could you use this agenda to organize what you are going to say next week? And here are some slides that I had my people create so you don't have to spend so much time drawing." The SME was very grateful for the help. "It would have taken me days to put this stuff together, and I just don't have the time. Thanks."

An important point from this story concerns having members of the target audience work with the SME to ensure that the audience gets the information it needs. I once worked with a telecommunications equipment manufacturer to put together a multi-day training program for its sales and sales support staff on a set of new products it was introducing to the market. All of the training was going to be done by the SMEs, in this case marketing, product management, and engineering personnel. I provided a half-day workshop on how to put together the training materials. I also gave each presenter the names and contact information for two people from the target audience who had agreed to work with them to help target the content to the needs of the audience. About half of the SMEs contacted their two audience resources, while the other half didn't bother - "We're the experts on these products. We know what they need." At the end of each session, we asked the audience to complete an evaluation questionnaire for the session. On a 5-point scale, those SMEs who had worked with the audience resources ahead of time scored an average of 4.4. Those who didn't use the audience resources in developing their sessions scored an average of 3.7 -- a very statistically-significant difference.

Another reason for involving members of the target audience in the development of the training program: they can help the SMEs avoid including material (and therefore wasting precious training time) that isn't needed.

I once developed a seminar on managing virtual teams. I had recruited an external consultant who was an expert on the subject matter to work with an instructional designer. The SME's typical consulting engagement included several hours of presentation to his client's executives on why the topic was important. Because we had not included potential audience members on the development team, we followed the lead of the SME in devising the agenda. When we piloted the seminar, the audience told us that the two hours we spent on why virtual teams were important was wasted. "If we weren't already convinced of the importance of virtual teams, we wouldn't have signed up for the seminar," they told us. So, we had to revise the content after the pilot, wasting time and money.

Most training groups have to rely on SMEs to help them learn the material they will be training or to actually do the training themselves. But, as discussed above, the training group can add great value to the training process by working closely with the SMEs.

A final note on using SMEs – often, the people who are closest to the work are better SMEs than the people who are thought of as experts. Here are several examples.

- While working on a new sales training program, I was told that the company's competitive analysis group was the one and only source for the competitive information that sales reps needed. After working with the group, I developed a three-level model for competitive information:
    - Company to company comparisons: How does your company stack up against the competition in categories such as age of company, financial stability, quality ratings, etc. For these types of comparisons, the competitive strategy group is the right group to act as SMEs.
    - Product to product comparisons: How does your company's product compare with your competitors' product in terms of cost, reliability, features and benefits. Again, the competitive strategy group should have all the information you need for your programs.
    - Sales strategies that work: Here, you are dealing with how successful sales reps have beaten the competition to get the

order. Here, it is those successful sales reps, not the competitive strategy group, who are your best SMEs.

- When I worked at Digital Equipment Corporation, the company's major competitor was IBM, and many of IBM's longstanding customers wouldn't even consider talking with our sales reps. The sales training organization, as part of its annual cycle of regional and national sales meetings sponsored a competition for the best 90-second "elevator speech" to get DEC's foot in the door. At each regional meeting, every sales rep presented his or her best 90-second speech. At the national meeting, the regional winners competed for the grand prize. I attended the national competition and was amazed and delighted with the creativity I witnessed. The outcome of the competition wasn't just a grand prize winner, but an effective way of having the sales reps learn from each other. The speeches were more creative and more effective than what the sales training group could have created.
- A third story is one I collected from a manufacturing company whose major product (80 percent of its sales) was making machine guns for the U.S. Department of Defense. In the second year of a five-year contract, the company was manufacturing 150 units per month. One day, the company was contacted

by the program manager from the Pentagon. Could they increase production to 200 or more units per month?

The vice president of manufacturing spent time examining the manufacturing process to see if they could increase production and found one bottleneck – a high-tech "milling and drilling" center which took blocks of metal and after milling and drilling created the framework onto which all of the other components were attached. This work center appeared to be working at capacity, and if they wanted to increase production, they would have to invest $500,000 to create a second work cell. He really didn't look forward to asking the CEO for this large investment, so he assembled an expert group (his own two industrial engineers, consultants from the manufacturers of the equipment, and the program manager from the Department of Defense), sent the work team off to another part of the factory for an afternoon, and had the experts try to figure out how to meet the new demand. Their answer was that they could probably get production up to 175 or 180 units a month, but 200 would be impossible without the investment in the second work cell.

The vice president decided to wait a few days before approaching the CEO with the request for capital funds. The next morning, as he was walking past the work cell, one of the employees from that cell stopped him. "Who were all the big shots here yesterday? What's the problem?" The vice president explained the situation. The employee thought for a couple of minutes and replied, "You know, I think we could get production up to 200 units – with some changes." The vice president replied, "Really?" (He didn't think it was possible, but he wanted to believe.)

"You know," said the employee, "I was down at the mall the other night, and I saw some really nice baseball jackets. Do you think if we got production up to 200 units, you might spring for new jackets for the members of the cell, maybe with the company logo embroidered on them?" The vice president said, "Sure, I could do that."

On Saturday morning, all six of the employees from that cell were in the factory. Four of them spent the weekend rearranging and fine-tuning all of the equipment in the cell. The other two spent the time rewriting the numeric-control programs for each piece of equipment. On Monday morning, the cell was back up and running and in the next 30 days the cell produced 230 units.

The point here is that the people who are closest to a problem often can come up with the best solution to the problem. This is why they should always be included in the planning of any training solution.

Let's look at each of the three components of Question 1.

- What Needs to Be Learned? -- This is the focus of most training groups, i.e., what people need to learn, whether that is a hard skill, a soft skill, a new procedure, etc. Most training groups do a good job with this part of the question.
- When? -- How fast does the training need to be developed and delivered? This can have a great effect on the development and delivery methods you choose for the training. In the case of the inventory system discussed earlier, the system was ready to use, and the CFO didn't want to wait four or five months for the vendor to develop an e-learning program. In many cases, when the training group receives a training request and asks when the training is needed, the answer will be "yesterday." But we need to live in the real world, and developing and delivering training in most cases cannot be done overnight. At the same time, traditional methods may take longer than I feel is really necessary.

When I worked at DEC, its Educational Services organization had a longstanding methodology. Training on a new product using

the standard methodology took 12 to 18 months to develop. This worked adequately when the development cycle for a new minicomputer was three to five years. But when new network products were being developed in six to nine months, the standard methodology wouldn't work. That is why I proposed a new approach which, as I said, was rejected by the Educational Services group, resulting in my going to work for the marketing group where I was not constrained by the standard methodology.
- Who Needs to be Trained? -- The size and geographic distribution of your target audience should figure prominently into your strategy for developing and delivering training. Should you invest the same level of resources in training that will be needed by twenty people who are all in the same location compared to training that is needed by 1,000 people scattered across the globe? Your training strategies must consider how large your audience is and where it is located. These considerations lead us to the next question in Part II of the Learning Contract.

Question 2: What Learning Methods Will You Use?

While there is a whole raft of learning methods available, ranging from traditional instructor-led classroom training to e-learning, distance learning, micro-learning, etc., you should remember that the great majority of corporate training programs still use the traditional classroom approach. Your choice of learning methods should depend not just on the answers to the first question in this section, but even more on the content of the training.

For example, if you need to train someone on making effective presentations, you can provide self-paced learning on such topics as how to create a presentation, how to arrange its content, how to develop slides or other support materials, etc., but the actual skills for speaking in front of an audience, interacting with that audience, reading audience reactions, and so on cannot be taught by e-learning – to be done effectively, they require that a person get up and give a presentation to an audience and get feedback from that audience, to be videotaped and to watch that video with a coach. If you need to minimize time off-the-job for participants, you might take a blended learning approach, providing self-paced materials for the first topics followed by a live class for the latter topics.

At the same time, e-learning can be very effective for factual learning. For example, learning how to read a company's annual report, how to write computer code using a particular tool, how to enter data into a company system, etc. can be done effectively with e-learning, assuming that you create a proper learning environment for such learning.

When I founded the virtual corporate university to train thousands of employees to achieve a variety of technical certifications, the training was delivered via e-learning courses from a major vendor. When I took several of the courses myself, I didn't like them. But, at the same time, they worked for the great majority of the company's employees. That is, the employees who took the courses passed the exams, the lesson being that you shouldn't let personal biases influence your choice of training methods.

Here is a set of questions to ask when choosing a learning method:

1. *Is any type of training or learning activity really going to solve the problem the company is facing?* This may appear to be an obvious question, but it is not asked often enough. Remember the examples at the end of the last chapter where training solutions were requested when the problem could not be solved by training.
2. *Can the needed topics of instruction be defined for the vast majority of the target audience, or will the success of the learning activity greatly depend on the ability of an instructor to adapt*

the content to audience needs in real time? Involving a few people from the target audience in your development efforts can help you to answer this question.
3. *How much value comes from the personal interaction of the participants with an instructor or with other members of the class?* This can be of prime importance in dealing with training that is meant to change behavior, such as presentation skills, communication skills, conflict resolution skills, or coaching skills.
4. *How much hands-on experience is required for the employee to master the learning content?* This can sometimes be accomplished through simulations; other times, it requires actual hands-on experience.
5. *What is the size and geographic distribution of the target audience?* (as discussed earlier)
6. *What is the cost of creating a self-paced learning solution versus that of a traditional instructor-led classroom solution?*
7. *How quickly does the training need to be done? How long will its value last before needing to be revised or before it is abandoned?*
8. *What technology is available to support the learning activities? How accessible is that technology to the target audience?*
9. *What resources are available to reinforce learning as employees apply their learning to*

their jobs? (This will be discussed at greater length in the next chapter.)
10. *How will the target audience respond to your chosen training method?* Even the best training program will have no value if the target audience doesn't use it.
11. *What if you did no training of any type on the topic? How would people learn what they need to do their jobs?* We'll discuss this more later in this chapter.

The focus of your training group should not be exclusively on developing and delivering training programs. Employees at all levels have a wide range of learning opportunities every day as part of their jobs. Those learning opportunities certainly include the training programs your group provides but extend well beyond your group's offerings.[2] To be truly effective in the learning role, your training group must extend the scope of its work beyond the design and development of training to become *learning facilitators*.

Training versus Learning Facilitation[3]

The title of this book is "On-Target Learning," not "On-Target Training." I have always viewed

---

[2] See Daniel R. Tobin, *Learn Your Way to Success*, McGraw-Hill, 2012
[3] Adapted from Daniel R. Tobin and Margaret S. Pettingell, *The*

myself as a *learning facilitator* rather than as a *trainer*. Let's look at the differences between the two roles.

Traditionally, trainers did training – delivering in a classroom a workshop, course, or seminar that he or she or another member of the training staff developed. Once the learning event was over, the trainer's responsibility ended. There may have been a "smile sheet" evaluation at the end of the program which asked if the trainer was knowledgeable in the subject matter, he or she responded well to participants' questions, or whether the training was worthwhile.

Today, being this type of trainer is not enough. We need to redefine the role of the trainer (and re-train the trainer) to become more of a "learning facilitator."

- *A trainer* determines what others need to learn, develops a training program to transmit the required knowledge and skills, and provides the training. *A learning facilitator* helps employees identify their personal learning needs and assists them in finding ways to satisfy those learning needs.
- *A trainer* develops training programs. *A learning facilitator* provides a variety of learning methods to help the employee meet personal and organizational goals.

AMA Guide to Management Development, AMACOM, 2008

- *A trainer* presents the training he or she has developed (or which has been obtained from an internal or external training developer). *A learning facilitator* enables individual and organizational learning from a wide variety of sources (not limited to the offerings of the training group).
- *A trainer* creates generic training programs for large audiences. *A learning facilitator* tailors learning solutions to meet individual and organizational learning needs.
- *A trainer* is focused on the acquisition of individual knowledge and skills. *A learning facilitator* is focused on the application of knowledge and skills to the job.
- *A trainer* is focused on the goals of the training program. *A learning facilitator* is focused on the goals of the organization and the organization's employees.
- *A trainer's* responsibility ends when the employee leaves the classroom or when he or she makes available an e-learning or other self-study program. *A learning facilitator's* responsibility ends when the employee has completed a learning activity AND has successfully applied that learning to his or her job.
- *A trainer* measures success by how satisfied the employee is with the training experience. *A*

learning facilitator measures success by how effectively learning is transferred to the job to make a positive difference in individual and organizational business results.

Let's look at a few examples from my own experience.
- My manager, the VP of human resources, told me that a senior engineering manager was going to be appointed vice president of marketing. Could I develop a plan to get him up to speed on marketing so he could get off to a running start in the new position. I found several week-long programs at local business schools that seemed very appropriate for this purpose. I printed out the brochures from the schools' websites and went to see him. He thanked me for the information but told me that he would prefer to find a business school professor who could provide him with a tutorial, give him books and articles to read and then discuss them with him one-on-one. I identified three candidates from local business schools, provided him with their biographies, and arranged for him to interview each one. He selected one and worked with him for more than a year with great success.
- I was contacted by the head of a family-owned construction company in the mid-West. The company had about 75 employees, was very successful, and had great opportunities to

expand. He had two young project managers that he wanted to groom into vice presidents. Could I develop a learning plan for them to facilitate their growth into the new positions? After spending two days with people at the company and interviewing the two project managers, I developed a learning plan for them that included an external course on negotiations skills and a structured apprenticeship with current vice presidents along with mentoring by the CEO.

- With DEC's Networks University, which I described earlier, my training group didn't develop a single one of the 40 to 70 sessions included in each program. We did provide design assistance to the subject-matter experts and training for them on how to put together their presentations.
- Because the Network University program was expensive, bringing hundreds of people together from all over the world for a week at a time, we initially designed it to utilize every minute of the day, with speakers at meals along with the many different sessions. The feedback we got was that the participants wanted more time to talk with each other and to learn from each other. As a result, we cut out most of the mealtime speakers and, one evening during the week, set up "birds-of-a-feather" sessions where different rooms at the conference center were assigned topics and a

moderator, and people could gather to exchange ideas and learn from each other. Because the participants were getting so much value from them, some of those sessions lasted well into the wee hours of the morning.
- As part of the overall Networks University program, we also set up what is today called a "community of practice." This was an intranet discussion forum where any member of the networks world could ask a question and get responses from people who had relevant knowledge and experience. For example, a sales rep in California once described a customer's computer facilities, including what machines they were using from various vendors, and asked for advice on creating a networking solution to tie them all together. Within 24 hours, the rep had advice and ideas from half a dozen people across the globe – people who he didn't know and who he probably couldn't have found on his own. This is another example of facilitating learning, rather than providing training.

Some years ago, I was presenting a session at Elliot Masie's annual conference in Orlando. Just prior to my breakout session, there was a great general session with a futurist who presented some great information for everyone in attendance. As I started my session, I asked the 200 people in my room "How many of you think that the last speaker had some great ideas for you?" Everyone's hand went up. "How many of you think that the information he presented would be of value to your CEO and other executives in your organization?" Most hands went up. "How many of you are planning to get a copy of the tape from the session or a copy of the speaker's book and give it to your CEO?" Two hands went up. *Being a learning facilitator means that you should be sharing your learning with anyone and everyone who could benefit from it!*

These are but a few examples of stretching beyond the traditional roles of designing and developing training programs that added great value to the company. Here are a few more ideas:

- Job Aids: Sometimes a job aid can provide all the information employees need to get the job done. In the case of the new inventory system discussed earlier, the job aid was a laminated card that listed the steps for registering each piece of equipment in the new system. Other job aids might be a similar "cheat sheet" or, for example, an outline of how to conduct a performance review. At a major industrial company, there was a problem with the quality of welding being done on parts from several subcontractors. To make it easier for the subcontractor to understand each problem, company created a set of samples that demonstrated various types of welding defects

and gave a set of these samples to each subcontractor. As a result, instead of trying to explain a problem on the phone, the company could say "Take a look at sample 12 – that's the type of defect we are seeing."
- Informal Learning: Studies have shown that the great majority of the learning that takes place within a company is done informally, that is, apart from formal training programs. For example, I once had to produce some charts from data I had assembled in a spreadsheet program. I had seen one of my colleagues produce some beautiful charts, so I asked him for a quick tutorial on creating charts from the spreadsheet program. In less than 30 minutes, he was able to teach me what I needed to know to get the job done. Otherwise, I would have had to sign up for a training program or spend hours with a manual trying to figure it out. Think about establishing a registry of subject-matter experts who would be willing to help other employees master new skills.
- Demonstrations: When we put together the Networks University program, one of the common requests from field personnel was to see the products at work – they were trying to sell products that they had never seen. So, as part of the Networks U program, we put together demonstrations of the technologies and products.

- Practicum: I once read a story from General Electric about a new manufacturing program they wanted to institute in a number of factories after it had been successfully piloted in one factory. The model to train the teams at the target factories included:
    o Each target factory sent a team of people to the pilot factory. The team included everyone who would be involved in the implementation process.
    o The team from the pilot factory provided training and demonstrations of the new program. The target teams then rotated through the various departments in the pilot factory to see in more detail how the program was implemented and to get answers to their questions.
    o At the end of these rotations, they met again as a large group. The facilitator went person by person through the pilot implementation team asking "What questions did these folks forget to ask? What more do they need to know?"
    o The teams from the target factories were then required to return to their home sites and implement what they learned, knowing that the people at the pilot factory were available to answer questions and troubleshoot any problems that might arise.

- Coaching: Sometimes, assigning a coach to help someone master a new skill will be more effective than sending that person to a training program. In one company for which I worked, there was one senior vice president who was known for "blowing his stack" at meetings whenever he disagreed with someone else's point of view. His behavior had become very disruptive. There were a number of excellent external workshops that we could have sent him to, but he was reluctant to take the time to attend them. Instead, we found him a coach to work with him on his communications style and it turned out to be a very effective solution. Think about establishing a registry of employees who would be willing to coach others on subjects that they have mastered themselves.
- Action-Learning Projects: One way to get people to start using their learning immediately is to assign action-learning projects where training participants are required to start using their learning as part of their jobs. As an example, many years ago, before the advent of Microsoft Project, my training group was hired by the company's internal information technology group to provide training on project management to 25 of its project managers using a third-party project management software package. We required the participants to bring to the class their project management notebooks – at the

time, this was the standard for project management in the group. In the class, they learned the new software package AND they were required to transfer all of the information in their notebooks into the new system and to start using the new system to plan the next steps in their projects.
- Attending an External Program: This can be very effective if there are only a few people who need training. But before sending someone to an external program, it is important to determine that the selected program is the right one for the job and to set the right expectations for the training, both before the program and when the participant returns from the program.

To be of optimal value to your company, you need to expand your thinking and your role in facilitating learning in any and all ways possible. Here are some other suggestions on how your training group can facilitate learning by employees. Let's take a quick look at each one and how your training group can facilitate these types of learning.
- Employees can learn from reading – reading books, reading articles in magazines and journals, reading information on websites, reading help screens on applications, etc.
- They can learn by observation. They can see how someone else is doing something and learn from it. They can even learn from poor

examples – if they see their manager doing something horrendous, they can make a note to themselves saying, "when I become a manager, I'm never going to do that to my people."
- They can learn from their mistakes by analyzing why something they did went wrong or produced an unacceptable result.
- They can learn from a coach who has been assigned to help them master some new skill or improve on a current skill.
- They can learn from attending a conference or trade show – learning how others approach problems and how others are using different methods.
- They can share their knowledge and experiences with each other using your company's intranet.
- The list can go on and on – there are many learning methods available to the individual employee.

So, how can your training group help employees learn from all of these methods, rather than just from the formal training programs that you create and offer? Here are some ideas:
- Publish learning resource guides -- Using the company's competency model, these guides list learning resources for each competency. If the company offers a training program related to the competency, that information is in the guide. But the guides go well beyond that. For

example, for any given competency, the guide lists some articles and websites where the employee can get more information; it may list college courses or distance learning courses that will help build the competency; if the competency is technical in nature, it may list subject-matter experts within the company who can be contacted to learn more about the competency. The guides may include suggestions for how to build the competency through practice and suggest how employees can do this.

- Because there are so many ways in which an employee can learn, the training group can offer assistance on learning how to learn. For example, it can produce a manual on informal learning methods (or distribute my book, *Learn Your Way to Success*). It can teach brainstorming skills so that employees can learn from each other and together as teams. It can teach employees how to efficiently search the web for information or how to use communities of practice within or outside the company to find answers. It can set up communities of practice on the company's intranet.
- Trainers can coach employees after they complete a formal training program to reinforce learning as employees try out their new knowledge and skills in their work.

- The training group can maintain a list of subject-matter experts who can act as coaches. It can also train managers and subject-matter experts within the company on coaching skills.
- If the company has, or wants to start a mentoring program, it can provide training to both mentors and mentees on how to use the relationship to learn from each other.
- The training group can sponsor "Lunch and Learn" sessions where subject-matter experts within the company can share their knowledge with others, either in a conference room in one location, or via a webcast.
- The training group can sponsor a book club, announcing the title of a business-related book each month and then leading a discussion on it – either a live discussion, a discussion via a web conference, or using a discussion forum. Any member of the club can recommend books for the group to read and then lead the discussion for that month.

The possibilities are endless – and every one of them can add value to the organization beyond the formal training programs your group offers.

As a training consultant, I have worked with many different organizations. Sometimes, I get a request for training that I can fill myself. Other times, I will know someone in my network who has a relevant program. And, sometimes, I don't have a clue where to find training on a topic of interest to my client or potential client.

One day, I answered my phone. On the other end was a training director for a racetrack and casino organization in a rural vacation area in the U.S. "I just read an article you wrote," he told me, "and I'm wondering if you could help me with a training need that has just arisen." I said I would try to help and asked him what the problem was he was trying to solve. He told me that he needed to provide training for employees in the casino on how to act when an armed robbery takes place.

Obviously, the casino had had an armed robbery and it hadn't gone well. Could I provide this training? No way! Did I have someone in my network who could provide such training? Not that I knew of. "Let me make some calls and see if I can find you a resource," I told him. "I'll get back to you by tomorrow with what I find out."

I made two calls. The first was to the state police headquarters in his state. The second was to the FBI. In both calls, I explained who I was and the training needed by the casino. Could they help? After getting bounced around to a few people in each agency, the answer from both groups was "Yes. We can do that. We have a program that we can deliver on that very topic. And we'll do it at no cost to the casino."

I called the training manager back. He was thrilled. He had spoken with his local police chief and the head of security at the casino, and neither of them felt able to do this type of training. The training director, himself, trained card dealers and slot machine mechanics, and had no idea what the training program should contain.

In this case, I was acting not as a trainer, but as a learning facilitator – finding the right learning resources to match the need of my client.

Question 3: Who will Develop any Needed Learning Materials?

You are your company's training group. It's your job to develop all training materials for the company. Right? Ask yourself these questions:
1. Do you have the subject-matter expertise needed to develop the training? If you do not have this expertise and must rely on an internal or external subject-matter expert, will it be more cost-effective to have your group member become a subject matter expert and then develop the training materials, or to have an instructional designer work with the designated subject matter expert to create the materials?
2. Do you have the instructional design skills needed for the delivery method you have selected? There is such a wide variety of tools, especially in the e-learning world, that it is unlikely that your staff can be expert in all of them. If you identify a tool that you think would

be effective in developing your learning solution, will it be more cost-effective to train a group member to use the tool or to find an external expert to help you?
3. Are there existing materials available from the vendor marketplace that can be used as is or adapted to meet the training need? There is a vast supply of packaged courses available from a variety of educational and commercial vendors. Can an external solution meet your company's training need more cost-effectively than creating an in-house solution? If you find an external resource that *almost* meets your need, can you adapt that resource so it fits better. (Remember how I had adapted the university course on Project Management and Control to meet the needs of my company.)

In examining the use of external materials, try to make certain that your internal audience will find the content relevant to their jobs. If the examples and case studies in the vendor's materials are not relevant to your employees' work, they will quickly lose interest. For example, having examples based on managing bank tellers will not gain or hold the participants' interest if your audience is primarily engineers or scientists.

You should view your job as a training group to meet your company's training needs, whether that means developing a training program yourself or bringing in an external program or some combination of the two.

Remember the inventory system training project we discussed earlier. In this case, the $100,000 solution proposed by the vendor was outrageously expensive. The learning solution we designed included the following elements, all created by the company's internal subject-matter experts with assistance from an instructional designer from my group.

- A one-page laminated instruction sheet for the vast majority of users.
- A two-hour webinar given by the company project manager and her staff for the super-users. The webinar was recorded so that people could access it whenever necessary to remind them of some aspect of the training or to train new super-users who would be appointed at a later date.
- The total cost for this solution was less than $5,000. And we delivered in in two weeks, rather than the four to five months that it would have taken to develop the e-learning program.

The choice of development method should also take into consideration how, and by whom, the training will be delivered, as discussed below.

Question 4: Who will Deliver the Needed Training?

Once you have settled on how you will develop a training program, you must also consider who will deliver that training.

- If you have settled on an e-learning program, you will need to get the company's IT organization involved. How will the programs be stored and accessed? Does the target audience for the training have access to the technology they will need to utilize the training? How much network traffic will be generated by people taking the training?
- If the training is to be delivered via a webinar or virtual classroom, do you want people to access it from their offices or do you want them to gather in groups in conference rooms or classrooms? Do you have the right equipment to broadcast and to receive the training?
- If the training is going to be led by an instructor or facilitator, who will that be? A member of your training staff? An external instructor or consultant? An internal or external subject-matter expert? A company executive or line manager?

Let's look at the alternatives for instructor resources and what each alternative means in terms of your development efforts.

- If the training will be delivered by a member of your training staff, what resources will he/she need to be most effective? Slides? An instructor guide? Instructional materials for the students? Job aids? If more than one member of your staff will be delivering the training, how do you ensure consistency and level of quality for each session? If your training staff will deliver a program that you have purchased from an external vendor, does the vendor provide an instructor's guide? Does the vendor offer a train-the-trainer program?

  At one company where I was the sole training resource, we wanted to train managers on coaching skills. After reviewing program materials from a dozen different vendors, I selected one vendor and enrolled in its train-the-trainer program. I then delivered the program to managers throughout the world – fifteen different sessions on three continents, training more than 200 managers. Once I had completed the train-the-trainer session, my only obligation to the vendor was to purchase their materials for each student.

- If the training is to be delivered by a subject-matter expert, you should pay close attention to the course materials he/she plans to provide and offer to assist in the development of those materials. Subject-matter experts, as discussed earlier, tend not to be experts at training and

your training group can add great value in shaping their presentations and developing the needed instructional materials.
- If you are bringing in an external consultant or trainer to do the training, pay attention to the materials they plan to use. Make certain that those materials meet your standards. Also, make certain that your company will have the rights to use any materials or job aids that they provide. Also, I tend to use external trainers and consultants only when the training need is for a relatively small audience and is only needed one or a few times. If you need to train a lot of people over a long period of time, you don't want to become too dependent on the external resource – their schedule may not meet your scheduling needs, and what if that person disappears for whatever reason? When I have had a need for long-term training and had to use an external consultant or trainer, I've made certain that part of the agreement is to have the external person train someone in my company to take over the training responsibilities after the external person has delivered the training a few times.

In using external instructors, try to find someone who has worked in your industry to gain credibility with your audience. For example, as part of a leadership development program I designed, I wanted to include a session on creativity and innovation. There are many vendors in the marketplace for this type of training. But my audience consisted primarily of chemical engineers and I knew that a generic presentation on these topics would not hold their interest. So, I used my network and found a workshop on the topic given by the former head of the center for innovation of a major chemical company – the result was that the presenter had instant credibility with the audience.

Sometimes, in the role of a learning facilitator, it isn't necessary to develop or deliver any training at all, but just to enable employees to learn from each other. Here's another example from an earlier book. At a specialty chemical company, the company published the recommended use of each of the chemicals it produced as a guide for its sales reps. The company asked each sales rep to write up any case where a customer was using a chemical for a purpose that wasn't on the list. The idea here is that customers were much more creative and probably had thought of other uses for the chemicals. By sharing these cases with the full sales force, reps were able to gain new business by suggesting other uses for the chemicals.
- Some companies have found it very effective to have training delivered by company executives or line managers. For example, when Jack Welch was the CEO of General Electric, he

taught in the company's leadership programs hundreds of times. This can be a great strategy – when employees see a company executive taking the time to train them, they know the content is important and that they will be expected to apply what they have learned to their jobs. When company executives will deliver the training, you need to be especially careful in the development process to ensure that the executive is comfortable with the content and that they have everything they will need to deliver the training effectively.

I mentioned in the introduction to this book that I had a personal bias in favor of instructor-led, classroom-based training. Here is a list of the advantages I believe that instructor-led training has over e-learning:

Advantage #1: Focus

When employees attend an instructor-led training session in a classroom, they are better able to focus on what it being taught. Compared to participating in an e-learning session from their workplaces, they have fewer distractions -- people are not stopping by their office, their phone isn't ringing, they are not getting signals from their PCs that they have a new mail message, etc. They are therefore more able to focus on the live training than if they are taking any type of e-learning in their offices. I have seen too many instances where an employee clicks through e-learning screens while "multi-tasking" and are accomplishing little if any learning, although the company's learning management system may give them credit for completing the e-learning course.

E-learning advocates have recognized these problems and have attempted to resolve them by including frequent short quizzes or polls that require the participants to "pay attention," but the fact remains that there are many more distractions for the learner in an e-learning environment than in an actual classroom.

Advantage #2: Confidentiality

A good classroom instructor will create a safe environment for learning and get the participants to agree that anything that is said or done in the classroom is confidential ("What's done in the classroom stays in the classroom"). For example, in a management training class, a participant may want to discuss a specific problem he or she is having with a particular employee. In an e-learning environment, this isn't possible -- the manager may be leery of talking about a specific employee problem because he or she doesn't know who else is participating in the class and is worried about the discussion becoming known to that employee.

Advantage #3: Practice

Some of the better e-learning programs I have seen provide opportunities for practice of new skills via simulation exercises, and some of these simulations are very good. But they cannot duplicate having students in a classroom practice their newly-acquired skills while receiving feedback from the instructor and each other.

For example, I have taught coaching skills to hundreds of managers around the world. One feature of the program I presented was to have participants bring into the classroom a current or past problem on which they felt they could benefit from coaching themselves. During the class, they were coached by other participants, using what they were learning. When the participants saw that they were helped by coaching, they were much more likely to use the coaching techniques when they returned to the job. This experience cannot be duplicated with e-learning.

Does this mean that e-learning cannot be used to teach coaching skills? In fact, you can use e-learning to present much of the material that I taught in the classroom, for example, how to ask good coaching questions, how to set the proper environment for coaching, etc. But you cannot effectively duplicate the practice of those skills in an e-learning environment.

Advantage #4: Adaptability

A good instructor can adapt the training content to the specific needs of the participants in the classroom. For example, while a training program may focus on a full overview of a topic, members of the class may point out one specific area with which they continue to have problems. A good instructor will follow the lead of the class and help them find ways to solve that problem. With e-learning, there is little adaptability to address this type of issue.

Advantage #5: Individual Attention to Participant Needs

In a face-to-face instructor-led class, the trainer may notice that one or more participants is having specific problems, either in understanding some topic or in applying the learning to their particular situation. A good instructor will watch for signs of these problems and will offer to help those participants during breaks or after class. E-learning instructors can't read these types of body-language signs.

Advantage #6: Establishing a Dialogue

With asynchronous e-learning, there is no opportunity to ask questions of an instructor. Even with synchronous e-learning, participants may type a question for the instructor, but there is little opportunity to ask a follow-up question or to establish a dialogue with the instructor or with other participants. In many face-to-face classes, these types of dialogues, when they take place, can add a huge value to the participants by being able to dig deeply into a subject that interests the participants.

Advantage #7: Learning from Other Participants

In every class or conference I have ever attended, I have found that at least half the value I receive comes not from the training content (no matter how good it may be), but from my informal interaction with other participants, during the class, at breaks, or over lunch, dinner, or drinks. While on-line discussion groups can offer such opportunities for informal interaction, they cannot match the experience of interacting face-to-face.

Advantage #8: Building Personal Relationships

It is virtually impossible to build a personal relationship with an instructor or other program participants using e-learning, but it happens all the time with face-to-face instructor-led training. These relationships can lead to sharing experiences, job offers, personal coaching, and reinforcement as two or more people try out what they have learned on the job, and even to marriages (yes, I have a documented case).

Advantage #9: Breaking Down Silos

Getting people from different business units and functional groups together in a classroom can help to break down the silos that inhibit cross-unit dialogue and cooperation. At one company, a management training program that brought people together from different business units around the globe resulted in two managers from different business units developing an idea that resulted in a new business unit that yielded hundreds of millions of dollars a year in new revenue, and the new business unit could not have been created by either of the business units alone. In many other cases, I have seen problems solved more quickly because a participant was able to get help from another person in a class instead of sending a request up through his business unit, across the top level to another unit, and then down that hierarchy to get the help that was needed.

Advantage #10: Building a Personal Network

This is an adjunct to the previous advantages of breaking down silos and building personal relationships. For example, in a leadership development program I designed and led, we brought together 36 high-potential mid-level managers from multiple business units, geographies, and functional areas. At the end of the first session of this program, several participants remarked that even if there had been no educational content, just having the opportunity to build a network with the other participants would have been worth the company's investment in bringing them together for several days.

There is no doubt that e-learning can be an effective training method for specific topics. But the e-learning zealots who argue that all classroom training can and should be replaced by e-learning are overlooking the many unique benefits of bringing together a group of employees in a classroom. I am certain that there are other advantages I have failed to mention, just as I am aware that the capabilities of e-learning tools continue to improve and can provide effective instruction for many subjects.

I should also mention that I have sometimes provided access to e-learning programs on subjects that I know would be more effectively taught in a classroom. The reason for this was to make available at least some access to learning materials to employees who are located remotely or in areas where there are not enough potential students to justify providing a local instructor-led program.

Question 5: How will You Ensure that the Needed Learning Takes Place?

This is a tough question. When I established the virtual university to help employees achieve a variety of technical certifications, the measure of learning effectiveness was whether the employee, after completing the training, could pass the vendor's certification exam. Similarly, you can create a test to be taken at the completion of any training program to determine whether the participant has learned the material presented in the program. What you need to watch out for here is that learning to pass the test is not necessarily the same as learning to do the job.

In talking with a program manager in one of my company's divisions about technical certifications, he told me that he had had to hire 30 people to staff a new government contract. He said that 80 percent of the applicants had listed a certain technical certification on their resumes. "More than half of those applicants wouldn't have known how to turn on a personal computer," he told me. "They had spent a lot of money with a variety of training companies who taught them how to pass the exams – not how to do any useful work."

So, how can your training group ensure that learning actually takes place? The first requirement is one that many training groups overlook, and that is setting the expectation for your participants they will learn what is being taught. If the learners do not come into your learning activity with the mindset that they are there to learn what is being taught, they won't give it their full attention and won't be engaged in the learning process. This is true whether they are in a classroom or taking some type of e-learning or other self-paced learning.

Who should set this expectation? Certainly, your trainer should start every class by previewing what people are expected to learn. If it is an e-learning program, the first few screens should set this expectation. At the same time, it is important to remember that the employees who take part in your learning activity don't report to you, and you don't write their performance evaluations. So, the person who should set the expectation that their job in taking the training is to learn the content and then use it in their jobs after the training is each employee's manager.

Very few managers take the time to set expectations before their employees take training. How can you get them to do this, especially when many of the managers don't really know what the training entails and may not themselves be experts in the subject matter? Here are a few strategies you can use:
- One week to 10 days before the training starts, send an email to each participant's manager that asks them to meet with the employee before the training starts and to set the expectation, both for

what the manager expects the employee to learn and for how the manager expects the employee to apply the learning to the job. Attach a one-page description of the program that describes the expected learning outcomes so that the manager knows what expectations to set.
- If the training you are giving is brand new to the organization and, therefore, the managers probably know nothing about the content or how it can be used on the job, have the instructor or another subject-matter expert hold a briefing for the managers that will give them some background on the new techniques or technologies you will be teaching in the program. You can do this with a web conference that you record, so that those managers who cannot fit the actual briefing into their schedules can access the content at a time that is more convenient for them.
- If the subject matter is very complex and will require the managers to support its application and act as a coach for the employees, you might want to schedule a separate training session and require managers to take that training before sending their employees.
- If you don't or can't expect the managers to coach employees as they apply their learning to their jobs, identify some subject-matter experts, including the instructor, who can act as coaches. Failing this, you might suggest to managers that

they send two or more people from their groups to the training so that they can reinforce and coach each other as they apply their learning to their work.

Besides testing, here are a few other strategies I have used to ensure that learning has taken place.
- In a sales training seminar, we presented the class with a model for how to think about the benefits of new communications technologies. Based on the model, we required each participant to create a customer presentation that they would give to a specified customer – a customer who had not done business with the company in the past. We then sent emails to the participants' managers asking them to have each person make the presentation to the local sales team in preparation for using it with customers.
- Use simulations to test how well training participants have learned and can apply what they have learned in the class. At the low end, these can be simple practice exercises. For example, in a negotiations skills training, you can provide scenarios where participants can practice their skills and get feedback as part of the class. At the high end, they can be sophisticated computer-based simulations such as those used to train pilots or nuclear power plant operators.

Question 6: How will Learning be Reinforced After any Learning Event?

This is the final question in Part II of the Learning Contract and it is an area in which most training groups fall short. Too many trainers feel that their responsibility ends at the conclusion of a class or when an e-learning program is made available. As stated in my introduction to this book, I believe that more than half of the investment companies make in training is wasted because what is learned is never applied to the participants' work.

If you want to ensure that the learning initiatives you sponsor have real impact on the achievement of individual, group, and organizational goals, you need to help people as they start to apply their learning to their work. Otherwise, when someone faces a problem in applying their new knowledge and skills, they will often give up and revert to their old ways of doing things: "This new method is supposed to be better, but I'm not sure I can do it correctly. I know that the methods I have been using will get the job done. Maybe the old methods aren't as effective or efficient, but I know they work."

So, how can your training group ensure that what is learned is reinforced on the job after participants have completed their training? Here are a few ways you can try:
- In the pre-program email to the participants' managers, you asked the managers to set the

expectation that they would use what they learned. By briefing managers about the program ahead of time, or by training the managers first, they should take primary responsibility for reinforcing learning on the job.
- You could tell the learning participants that their trainer will be available by email to answer questions after the training takes place and promise a 24-hour turnaround on questions.
- You could set up a discussion forum on the company's intranet on the topic of the training and then get your trainers and other subject-matter experts in the company to monitor the discussions and answer questions.

The Virtual Follow-Up Session

A cost-effective solution for reinforcing learning from an instructor-led workshop or an e-learning program on the job is to conduct what I call a "virtual follow-up session." A virtual follow-up session is a 60- to 90-minute web conference or teleconference led by the instructor (for a live seminar) or a subject matter expert (for an e-learning program).

1. For an instructor-led seminar or workshop, schedule a virtual follow-up session for two to three weeks after the completion of the seminar. This also sets the expectation with the

participants that they will apply what they learn to their work. For an e-learning program, tell your target audience that you expect them to complete the program by a certain date and then schedule the virtual follow-up session two to three weeks after that date.
2. One week before the scheduled virtual session, survey the participants for questions, such as:
    a. "I thought I understood topic X in the seminar, but now that I am trying to apply it to my work, I find that I didn't understand it as well as I thought I did. Could you go through this topic again?"
    b. "Here's a question I didn't know to ask until I tried to apply what I learned to my work. Can you help me with the answer?"
    c. "I tried applying what I learned to my job, but I ran into this obstacle. Can you help me figure out how to overcome or get around this obstacle?"

3. Provide the results of your poll to the instructor or subject matter expert who will lead the virtual follow-up session so that he or she can prepare to answer the participants' questions.
4. On the appointed date, convene the web conference or tele-conference. You should have a separate person handle the logistics and keep track of questions that may come in during the

session, allowing the leader to focus on answering questions or providing additional instruction. Start by asking the participants what progress they have made in applying their learning to their jobs.

Virtual follow-up sessions are very low in cost because they can use the existing web conference or teleconference services supplied by your company. If your company doesn't have a contract with a provider of these services, ask your internal information technology or telecommunications group to make the needed arrangements to hold a session. If you want to try this and don't have a contract with a web conference company, most of those companies offer a free trial of their services.

Some common questions that arise concerning virtual follow-up sessions include:

- *What if the participants don't show up for the session?* My experience is that as you start with these sessions, participation often falls in the 33 – 60 percent range (but those who do participate find it very worthwhile). Most of the major web-conference services have a feature where you can record a session and make it available later to those who didn't participate. One effective strategy is to build the follow-up session into the plan for the learning program so that the expectation is set that the program isn't over until the follow-up session is completed. This also sets

the expectation with the learners that they will immediately apply what they have learned to their jobs, and that you will be checking on their progress.
- *Our instructors already have grueling schedules, and many of our learning programs are given several times a month – I'm worried that the logistics of having them available for these follow-up sessions will just be too much.* If this is your situation, you should consider holding one follow-up session every month or every quarter and invite all of the learners who participated in the live seminars or e-learning programs during that time to participate.
- *Our instructors have never given "webinars" or conducted web conferences and are fearful of making errors that will make them look foolish. And the folks who develop our e-learning programs just don't have good presentation skills. How can we make them effective in this new role?* There are a number of sources of training on how to make effective web presentations. Holding a mock session before going live can help them hone their skills and boost their confidence. The use of an experienced freelance webcast producer can also make the session go flawlessly.

The benefits from conducting a virtual follow-up session include:

- Better ensuring mastery of the material to be learned
- Better ensuring that what is learned in the classroom or from an e-learning program will be applied correctly to participants' work
- Better ensuring that you get a Kirkpatrick Level III or Level IV return on your investment in the learning program (see Chapter 5 for a discussion on evaluation methods).

Whether you use instructor-led classroom training or focus on using e-learning programs, holding virtual follow-up sessions can be a great, low-cost, addition to your learning arsenal to help ensure mastery and, more importantly, application to the participants' work to make a positive difference in individual and organizational business results.

When to Say "No" to a Training Request

Before ending this chapter on Part II of the Learning Contract on how to develop your learning plan, let me talk about one other topic: When to say "No" to a training request. For many training groups, saying no to a training request is never done, especially if the requester is willing to fund the effort. But to build your group's credibility in the organization, there are times when you absolutely should reject a training request.

The first circumstance when you should reject a training request is when you don't believe that the requested training will solve the problem. In my example of the state correctional system, if I had done the training that was requested, the problem wouldn't have been solved. By examining the roots of the problem, I was able to develop the right solution. In my example of the product manager wanting my group to develop and deliver sales training on his new product set, I found that the lack of training wasn't the source of the problem. Rather, the problem was that sales reps got no credit for selling the products. In both of these cases, responding to the original training requests would have been a total waste of time, effort, and resources (and would have done little to improve the reputation of the training group).

The second circumstance where you should turn down a training request is when the requestor won't provide the necessary time or attention to the training – something that happens too often. For example, a manager decides that the people in his or her group need training on some topic and they throw a request at your training group. When you ask the manager to work with your group to better define the training, or to provide subject-matter expertise, they say something like: "Look, training is your job. Just go do it, and don't bother me." To me, this also implies that the manager is unlikely to provide any support or reinforcement for the employees as they try to apply what they learn to their jobs, and this greatly diminishes your chances of success. Think of my example of the manager who requested that her employees attend team training when the real problem was a lack of team leadership on her part.

Here's an example from my experience. When I was the training director at a high-tech company, the vice president of engineering left the company and one of his direct reports was appointed as the new vice president. A few days later, he asked me to attend a meeting with him and his human resources business partner.

"Engineers are typically not good team leaders," he told me. "I want you to provide training for me and all my direct reports on team leadership." After discussing what he wanted to see in the program, I told him that I would put together a proposal for him by the end of the next day. I went back to my office and prepared a set of learning objectives and an outline for a two-day training program. I asked his HR business partner to review it before I passed it on to him. She came back to me and said it was a very good outline and that she was meeting with him the next and would review it with him.

The next day, she called me while she was meeting with him. "Can you do it one day?" she asked. "No," I replied, "but I could do one day of training and then do the second day a week or two later." She stopped by my office after her meeting.

"Here's the situation," she told me. "He's having all his direct reports come in for a week-long meeting next week. You'll have all day Friday to do the first day of training. Then, when they come back again next month, you can do the second day."

"That sounds workable," I told her, and I started developing the materials for the training.

On the next Monday afternoon, she called me from the meeting. "They have a lot on their agenda. We can only give you a half-day on Friday for the training. We'll do the rest next month when they are all back here." I wasn't pleased by this, but it was workable.

On Thursday morning, she called me again. "They are really running over schedule on all their agenda items. We can only give you from 2 to 4 PM on Friday, and half the people have to leave by 3:30 to catch their planes."

"No," I told her.

"What do you mean by 'No'," she asked.

"I set out a list of objectives for the training, and everyone will be expecting me to meet those objectives. They were based on two days of training, and now they are going to expect to meet those objectives in less than two hours. This is setting the training up for failure, and if I fail this time, there won't be a second opportunity. Tell them I am happy to do the training, but only when they have the desire to learn and are willing to set aside sufficient time for it."

She wasn't happy with my refusal, but it worked out well. When the engineering group came together the next month, they gave me two full days, on Wednesday and Thursday, and the training went well and met its objectives.

A third circumstance in which you should say no to a training request is when you can see that the larger change effort that the training is designed to support is missing other, non-training elements that will doom it to failure. This example came from a software company where a friend worked.

This software company constantly received complaints about its user support call center, such as:
- "I called with three questions. Your person answered the first question and quickly hung up before I could ask the other two."
- "Your person wouldn't spend the time to really understand my question."
- "All they told me was to look it up in the manual."
- And so on…

The company's reputation was on the line. They hired a new manager for the call center and the first thing she did was to bring in a three-day training program on customer service skills for all of the call center personnel. The results were outstanding. Almost immediately, the company was getting emails from its customers saying "I don't know what you did, but your call center is now a joy to work with. Your people are taking the time to make certain they understand my questions and then to make sure that I understand their answers. Fantastic! Keep it up!"

The positive changes lasted 17 days. On the 17th day after the training was completed, one of the call center reps was given her performance review. "I'm afraid that we won't be able to give you a raise this year," said her manager. "Your productivity has fallen off the charts."

"What do you mean?" asked the rep.

"I have your statistics here for the past two weeks. You know that our goal is to get each call answered in less than two minutes. For the past two weeks, you've been averaging three minutes and 22 seconds per call. So, I can't give you a raise."

It took less than an hour for everyone in the call center to learn that they were still being measured by the "less than two minutes" rule. Immediately, their old behaviors replaced the newly-learned behaviors.

The moral is that you need to ensure that new behaviors being learned in training are being reinforced on the job. Countless organizational change initiatives have had zero or negative results because companies have told their employees that they want them to behave in new ways but continue to measure and reward them for practicing old behaviors.

Learning Contract Part II – Summary

The purpose of Part II of the Learning Contract is to develop your learning plan based on the learning agenda generated in Part I. Training groups should look beyond traditional training techniques (while not abandoning traditional methods) for ways in which both formal and informal learning can enable and facilitate the achievement of organizational, group, and individual goals – they should move beyond training to new roles as learning facilitators.

Chapter 4

The Learning Contract Part III: Applying Learning to the Job

Part III of the Learning Contract deals with how employees will apply their learning to their jobs. Most training groups spend little if any time on this, feeling that their job is done once the employee leaves the classroom or once the e-learning product is made available. But if you want your efforts to actually have a positive impact on the achievement of organizational, group, and individual goals, you must follow through to ensure that your efforts add value to the organization. Here are the three questions to be answered in Part III of the Learning Contract:

- How will the employee apply the learning to the job?
- What reinforcement or assistance will be available to help in this application?

- What changes in organizational, team, or individual performance are expected to result from the learning?

Question 1: How Will the Employee Apply Learning to the Job?

It is the learners' managers who must set the expectation that they will use what they learn in their work, and this must happen before the learning takes place. You can reinforce this during the learning activity, but if the managers set this expectation before the class, you can be assured that the participants will pay more attention to the learning than if this expectation is not set beforehand. Here's an example from my experience.

When I led program design and development for the American Management Association, we created a new course called "Communicating with Tact, Diplomacy, and Credibility." The product manager first proposed this course as an advanced communications course – for people who were already good communicators but wanted to hone some advanced skills, and we designed the course for that purpose.

When we started giving the course, we found that we had a very different audience than we had planned for. The people who were being sent to the program were people who had very poor communications skills. In fact, many were sent because they were offensive in their communications and their managers were sending them as a last-ditch effort to save them from being fired. The real problem arose because the participants' managers had never told them why they were being sent, and, for most of them, they didn't recognize that they had a problem at all. And when they were told why they were there, they were offended, and some became hostile.

When we discovered who was coming to the course, we had to redesign it for this new and unexpected audience. We also sent a message with the registration confirmation asking the enrollees to hold a meeting with their manager, prior to the class, to discuss why they were being sent to this program. I also gave instructions to my team in revising the course that we needed to start the program with a statement like: "You are here because you are not good communicators. In fact, people in your workplace find it difficult to work with you. But we have both good news and bad news for you. The bad news is that if you don't do something about it, you may find your career opportunities very limited. You may also find yourself out of a job. The good news is that your employers value your skills enough that they feel you are worth saving and so they have sent you to this course. The even better news is that if you work with us in this course, we can help you."

Our training job with this course would have been much easier and effective if the participants' managers had had the courage to speak with them before sending them to course, to explain to them why they were being sent, and to set the expectation for what new and improved behaviors they were expected to master in the course.

Here's another example of how the lack of early (pre-training) involvement of the employee's manager can result in a waste of resources and no return on investment in training.

I once met with the vice president of power generation at a public utility. He told me that nine of the top eleven people in his business unit, including himself, were eligible to retire in the next five years and "I have no idea where we are going to find replacements for them."

I asked him if they had considered some type of leadership development program to prepare the next generation of leaders for the business. "I sent one guy to a very expensive leadership program for a week – nothing changed. A total waste of money!"

I spoke with Joe, the person who had attended the program. "It was a great program. I learned a lot, and I changed a lot. But I got back here and nothing else had changed, other than having a week's worth of work to catch up on. I suggested some new ideas to my boss, and he said that everything was working fine – no need for change. So, I'm really using nothing of what I learned."

Rather than make the argument here that the company should have built its own leadership development program, let's focus on how this utility company could have gotten more value from their investment in this individual. The program which this individual attended is well-known and highly-rated. The program itself was not at fault. What was missing from this attempt at developing a new leader was a lack of planning and preparation before the program as well as follow-up and follow-through after Joe returned from the program.

There are five steps that should have been taken in the planning and preparation for Joe's development:

1. Identification of Joe as having high potential for a future leadership role in the business unit
2. A 360-degree assessment to identify Joe's strengths and the areas in which he needed further development
3. Identification of a suitable executive education/leadership program for Joe
4. Preparation of Joe for that program and setting of expectations for what he would learn and how he would use his new learning when he returned from the program
5. Debriefing Joe when he returned from the program and developing an implementation plan for Joe

The process should have started with a conversation about Joe among the vice president of power generation, his HR director, and Joe's direct manager. The vice president obviously thought that Joe had the potential to grow into a leadership position. What did the others think? Based on Joe's job performance and on the qualities and competencies needed to lead the business unit, should Joe be labeled as a high-potential (Hi-Po)?

Assuming that Joe was designated as a Hi-Po, the next step should have been to conduct a 360-degree assessment of Joe to better identify his strengths and the areas in which he needed development. The results of the assessment should have been reviewed, first with Joe, and then in a meeting with the vice president, the HR director, and Joe's direct manager to reach agreement on the areas where Joe needed to develop new or improved competencies, resulting in a learning agenda for Joe.

Next, the HR director and Joe should have spent time researching the many programs available from business schools and other training providers. These institutions or companies all have counselors who could be called – "Here's what I need to learn and the skills I need to hone. What programs do you have that can meet my needs?" Beyond the counselor, they could also ask to talk with the program's faculty to learn more about the program and how it would address Joe's needs. Once the research was done, Joe and the HR director could choose the optimal program for Joe.

The final step that should have been taken before sending Joe to the program is a meeting involving Joe, the HR director, the vice president, and Joe's direct manager to set expectations for what Joe would learn and how he would use that learning when he returned from the program. "Here's what we expect you to learn from the program, and here's what we want you to do when you return." The post-program assignments could have included an expanded job description, a new job, a special project assignment, or another way of enabling Joe to apply his learning at work.

Given that there were a number of expectations set before sending Joe to the program, it is vital that the vice president follow up on those expectations and follow-through in enabling Joe to apply what he has learned to his work in preparation for larger leadership roles in the business unit and the company.

Once Joe returns from the program, the HR director, the vice president, and his direct manager should meet with Joe again to follow-up on their initial meeting. "Here are the expectations we had set before the program. How well did the program help you meet those expectations?" The meeting should also be used to reinforce the plan for Joe to use what he learned, either in his current job or in the new job or special assignment that had been agreed upon earlier.

This meeting is also an opportunity for Joe to tell the others, based on what he learned, what he plans to do in his current or new role and what support he will need to accomplish this from the three of them or from others. Based on this conversation, Joe should develop an action plan and a new set of goals against which they will measure his success.

It is then up to the vice president to follow through on the new assignment by meeting with Joe on a regular basis to check on his progress and to develop a sense of when he will be ready for a larger leadership role in the business unit and the company.

Had this vice president followed these steps, he, the company, and Joe would all have reaped many more benefits from this investment in Joe's development, and Joe would have been on track for a future leadership role in the business unit and in the company. As it happened, Joe started looking for another job outside the company because he was so frustrated, so the vice president was right in saying that it was a total waste of money.

Part III of the Learning Contract requires the early involvement of the participants' managers so that they have the time to set their employees' expectations of how they will use what they learned. Further, it requires a commitment from the managers that they will support the utilization of the training on the job once the training is completed. While this is the third part of the Learning Contract, it requires your training group to work with management well before any training takes place.

At the same time, there are steps your training group can take to facilitate the utilization of the training content in people's work. What do you, as the learning designer or as a trainer, need to know about how the subject matter will be used by your participants in their work? The answer is that you must become familiar with the application of what you are teaching. Only by understanding how the learning content will be used after the class can you ensure that the learning activities you design will be relevant to your participants.

Here are a few ideas you may find helpful.

- Are you developing training on a new system, process, or procedure for a particular group of employees? Ask the group's manager if you can spend some time observing how the group's work is currently done. By doing this, you can better understand how the training you will develop will be implemented and how it will change the work of the group's employees.
- As suggested earlier, in working with a subject-matter expert, try to include one or two people from the target audience in the development of the training. This will help you focus on how your training will actually be applied. If the target population finds your training relevant to their work, if they feel that it will add value, they

are more likely to use it after the training is completed.
- Check in with people who attended your training program to see how they actually implemented what they learned. If they didn't implement it, try to determine whether the lack of implementation is due to some problem with the training or stems from some other cause, such as lack of manager support or some other element that is missing from the overall change initiative. If the problem stems from the training you provided, see what you can do to remediate the situation immediately as well as what you need to do to revise the training for the next cohort so that it can be applied more easily the next time.

Often, when you find that training has not been applied to the job, the problem will stem from the employees' fear of change. "I know this new way is supposed to be better, but I'm uneasy about it. The old way may not be as good, but it works, and I know how to use it, so I'll just keep doing it the same old way and get the job done. I don't want to start making mistakes!"

Further, your training group can plan to provide on-going assistance after training takes place, which leads us to the next question in the Learning Contract.

Question 2: What reinforcement or assistance will be available to help in the application of learning to the job?

As stated earlier, many trainers feel that their job is done once employees leave the classroom or when they have delivered an e-learning program. But if you want to ensure that the training your group creates makes a real difference to the achievement of organizational, group, and individual goals, your involvement must extend beyond the classroom. So how can your training group provide such reinforcement and assistance? Here are a few ideas to consider:

- Provide job aids, such as a one-page set of instructions, a small model of a new process, or other tools that provide reinforcement on the job and assist in the implementation of new processes or procedures.
- Set up a discussion forum on your company's intranet so that people can ask (and answer) questions and reinforce each other as they implement what they learned. Promise that the instructor or a subject-matter expert will monitor the forum to answer questions.
- Brief participants' managers on what was covered in the course and what help and reinforcement they may need to provide to their employees as they implement what they learned.

- Set up a "buddy system" – ask participants to pair up with others so that they can coach and reinforce each other as they implement what they have learned.
- Schedule a Virtual Follow-Up Session as described in the last chapter.

A "Perfect" Model for Follow-Up

Perhaps the best model I have seen for training follow-up came from a small metal-crafting company in Canada. This was a low-tech industry that made chains for chain saws. The company wanted to institute statistical quality controls into its manufacturing processes and hired two experienced engineers/statisticians to lead the effort.

These engineers developed a two-day training program for intact work groups, including the work group foreman. Following the two days of classroom training, the engineers worked on the shop floor with the work group to apply the classroom learning to the job. By the end of the week, the work group was able to use what they learned to improve their work flow and results, allowing the instructors to move on to help other groups.

Question 3: What Changes in Performance are Expected?

The final question to be answered in Part III of the Learning Contract is: "What changes in organizational, team, or individual performance are expected to result from the learning?" This is the ultimate question and while it appears as the last question in the Learning Contract, the answer has to come from the beginning of the process.

A major tenet of program planning is that the goals of the program must specify the expected outcomes. That is, the expected changes in performance must be specified in the program goals. If you don't specify those measurable goals up front, it will be very difficult to justify the investment in learning after the fact. In the next chapter, we will discuss the evaluation of learning initiatives in greater detail.

Frequently-Asked Questions About the Learning Contract

As I have presented the concept of the Learning Contract to groups around the world, there are three questions that commonly arise:
1. Does this have to be a real contract, signed by all parties? The Learning Contract is a process, rather than a formal document.

2. At what level (corporate, team, or individual) can you use a Learning Contract? The process can be useful for planning learning initiatives at all levels of an organization.
3. What if we don't get the results specified in the Learning Contract? You will need to go back to your original analysis in Part I of the Learning Contract to diagnose why the expected results were not achieved – you should not presume that the failure to achieve the desired business results is automatically a failure of the training process.

Chapter 4: Summary

Part III of the Learning Contract deals with how learning gets applied to the job to make a positive difference in organizational, group, and individual performance on business goals. This is an area that training groups tend to ignore, but it is the ultimate evaluation measure for any learning initiative. The key here is that all three of the questions in Part III must become an integral part of the training group's planning process. If you don't include these considerations in your original plan, it will be difficult, if not impossible, to justify the investment in training *post facto*.

Chapter 5

Evaluating Your Learning Initiatives

As I discussed in the last chapter, the ultimate evaluation measure for any learning initiative is whether it helped the organization, and groups and employees within the organization, meet their individual and collective business goals. I have long argued that trying to prove the value of a learning initiative based solely on the costs and direct returns on the investment in that initiative is NOT the correct evaluation method, as I will explain later in this chapter.

The "Smile Sheet" Evaluation

I started working for Digital Equipment Corporation (DEC) in 1981. As I have described earlier, DEC's educational services organization had long-established methodologies for everything from how to write a question for a needs assessment to the font style and size to use in student materials. At that time, DEC's courses were typically five days long and covered everything a field person needed to know about one of the company's computers – from how to configure the computer in developing a customer proposal to how to install and repair it. The methodology also included a standardized end-of-course evaluation sheet. Commonly known as a "Smile Sheet," this 20+ item questionnaire asked about the quality of the materials, the comfort of the training center, the knowledgeability of the instructor, etc. The "smile sheet" gained this name because it measured how happy the participants were with the training experience. At DEC, instructors were measured and rewarded based on the ratings they received and they quickly learned how to ensure that their ratings were high, even if the participants weren't particularly happy with the course. It did nothing to measure whether the participants found the course useful for their jobs or whether it added any value to their work. Remember that this was in the early 1980s, and the Kirkpatrick 4-Level Model wasn't well known at that time.

The R-V-Q Evaluation Model

When I created Networks University, with 40 to 70 different sessions offered over five days, I wanted

to measure more than just the "happiness" of the participants. I also didn't want to deal with 40 to 70 different sets of 20+ question smile sheets. So, what did I want to measure? I came up with a three-question survey for each session. Participants were asked to rate each session on:
1. Relevance (R) – Will you be able to use the information imparted in the session immediately upon returning to your job?
2. Value (V) – Will the content of the session add value to your job? By "value" I mean will you be able to do something faster or better or at reduced cost based on what you learned?
3. Quality (Q) – This category covered the types of questions typically found on the smile sheet – the quality of the presentation, the knowledgeability of the presenter, the facilities, etc.

If a session could meet these three criteria, I judged it a good session. The R-V-Q model actually inspired the Learning Contract model on which this book is based.

The Kirkpatrick Model[4]

Today, I believe that the Kirkpatrick 4-Level Model is the gold standard for training evaluation.

---

[4] While there has recently been some discussion as to the origin of the 4-level model of evaluation, I refer to it as "The Kirkpatrick Model" because the work and books by Don

(Later in this chapter, I will explain why I don't believe in doing return-on-investment, or ROI, evaluations for training programs.) Let's examine how the Learning Contract, and the RVQ model relate to Kirkpatrick's four levels:
- Level 1: Reaction
- Level 2: Learning
- Level 3: Behavior
- Level 4: Results

Kirkpatrick's Level 1 is Reaction. The criteria for this level are those that typically appear on smile sheets or, in the R-V-Q model, the "Quality" rating.

Kirkpatrick's Level 2 is Learning – did the learning participants master the content presented in the program. This measure can be done through a test or through simulations where participants demonstrate their mastery of the content. The R-V-Q model does not deal explicitly with this criterion. In the R-V-Q model, it is assumed that if the participants find the content relevant (R), and if they feel it will add value (V) to their jobs, they will learn it. The real measure of learning in the R-V-Q model is whether the learning content gets applied to people's jobs.

Kirkpatrick and, more recently, by Jim and Wendy Kirkpatrick have popularized the model and provided excellent explanations and applications of the four levels.

Level 3 is Behavior – after completing the learning activity, do participants change their behavior and actually use what they have learned. This is also covered in the R-V-Q model, since if the participants find the content relevant to their jobs and find that it has value to them in their work, their behavior will certainly change.

Level 4 is Results – what changes as a result of learning. The measure of this in the R-V-Q model is Value – has the learning resulted in improved business results at the individual, group, and organizational level?

Learning is Typically Just One Part of the Solution

It is vital to remember that in Part I of the Learning Contract, you started with business goals and then diagnosed what needed to change to meet those goals. Those changes might include everything from new product development to organizational redesign to changes in pricing strategies, to the development of new systems and procedures. Once you knew what needed to change, you then asked what needed to be learned in order to make those changes, so learning is typically only one part of the solution. If the other parts of the solution are not implemented, and if the organization does not have what I call a "positive learning environment," it is very unlikely that even the best learning solution will produce the desired business results. Therefore, I conclude, it doesn't make sense to evaluate the return on investment in a learning solution based solely on the results of a training program. For example, if a company's manufacturing facilities are totally out-of-date, there is very little that a training program can do to reduce the cost of manufacturing. In the earlier example of the product line that wasn't selling because sales reps got no credit for selling those products, providing more sales training on those products would not have increased sales. Similarly, in my example of the state correctional system, the problem was a lack of leadership and the requested solution of teaching Senge's "five disciplines of the learning organization" would not have solved the problem.

ROI Is NOT the Right Evaluation Measure for Training Programs

There are many advocates of using return on investment (ROI) calculations as a measure of training effectiveness. I disagree with this approach. My primary objection to ROI evaluation of training is that it is virtually impossible to isolate the monetary benefits of a training initiative. Looking again at Part I of the learning contract, the analysis of what needs to change in order to meet business objectives, it is rare that training is the only part of the solution. While it is easier to measure the costs of training, as compared to costs of, for example, organizational redesign, it is not easy to isolate the benefits of training from the overall benefits of the change solution.

I often use the analogy of a car manufacturer that is planning a new model. In planning for the new model, there are many costs to be included, from re-tooling manufacturing systems to labor costs to parts costs, etc. The manufacturer does not ask the department in charge of wheels and tires to do a return on investment calculation to justify putting wheels and tires on the new car – everyone knows that you can't manufacture a new car without wheels and tires. The manufacturer does do ROI calculations to justify the new model, but those calculations are done on the total costs of building the new model versus the anticipated revenues from that model.

Similarly, ROI can be useful in evaluation of an overall change initiative, but it doesn't make sense to try to isolate whether the training component of that initiative will generate more of the return than a change in organizational design or the retooling of a factory. In fact, when business schools teach ROI, it is always used to evaluate future proposals. If an organization has three different investment proposals under consideration, ROI is used to evaluate which of those proposals promises the greatest financial returns to the organization. ROI is NOT used to evaluate completed projects.

As a side note here, I have seen too many cases where ROI analysis has been used to justify developing an e-learning program. The argument states that if we can save travel expenses for bringing employees to a class as well as the cost of instructors and facilities, these savings are benefits to the organization. In too many cases, these types of justifications have been made with little regard to how much learning will actually take place from the e-learning solution versus an instructor-led, classroom-based solution. This is not to say that e-learning cannot be a very effective learning solution in some cases. But one error that many organizations make is assuming that because a solution is e-based, employees need no time to dedicate to learning. There are numerous sci-fi novels where chips are implanted in people's brains so that learning can be instantaneously downloaded, but these novels usually end in tragedy.

Tangible versus Non-Tangible Benefits of Learning

Over the course of many years, there has been a lot of discussion about how to evaluate the effects of "soft skills" training, e.g., management and leadership skills, communications and conflict management skills, etc. Some have tried to use ROI analysis to prove their worth – for example, if we train managers can we reduce employee turnover and, therefore, count as the benefits from the training the reductions in talent acquisition costs?

I am reminded of an experience I had many years ago. I became involved in the planning of a new religion-affiliated private day school. I, along with many other parents of potential students, was a member of the group that was to define the charter for the new school. As the committee started its discussions, all of the parents were focused on the educational goals for their children. While this was the core requirement for the charter, I reminded the committee members that there needed to be a lot more to the charter than just educational goals. For example, what role would parents play in the school? What would be the relationship of the school to the religious institutions that were sponsoring and supporting it? What role should the school play in the community in which it would be located? What type of working environment did they want to establish for teachers and staff?

Similarly, when an organization defines its goals, it needs to look beyond profit ratios and returns on investor capital. What are the company's values? What kind of culture does it want to build? How does it want to treat employees? What role does it want to play in the communities in which it works? These are all "intangibles," but, at the same time, they are very tangible – look at the effects on organizations from the Me-Too movement or the effects on lack of community involvement from Amazon's decision to build (and then not to build) a headquarters in New York City.

When I designed a leadership development program (LDP) for 36 mid-level managers in a high-tech company, I listed the expected results of the program as follows:

1. Through a comprehensive set of educational sessions focused on the company's key competencies, the LDP will help participants develop the leadership skills, business acumen, and execution skills they will need when they assume new leadership roles.
2. The company will expand and improve the quality of its bench strength and have a larger pool of qualified talent available when developing the company's succession plans.
3. The company will retain some of its top talent that it might not otherwise have kept – employees who see that the company is investing in their future with the company are more likely to stay.
4. Through action-learning projects, the company will solve some longstanding company challenges that might otherwise never have been addressed.
5. Through those action-learning projects, the company will be able to test the readiness of

participants to take on larger roles, thereby avoiding potentially costly promotion errors.
6. The LDP will make visible to the company's executive team a wide range of talent that they might otherwise never have seen.
7. The company will see participants improve their performance in their current jobs as a result of what they learn in the LDP.

Not many of these benefits are tangible in the sense that we could place a dollar value on them, but they nonetheless added great value to the organization.

Correlation versus Causation

Many studies over the years have shown that the most successful companies generally spend more on training than less successful companies. This is a correlation. We have no evidence that says that the larger training budgets of successful companies is the *cause* of their success (as much as we wish this could be so). It may just be that more successful companies have more money available to spend on training.

I have often been asked, mostly by people new to the learning and development field, how much money per employee a company should be spending on training, or how many days of training per year an organization should provide to its employees. State-of-the-industry reports focus on these types of statistics because they are easy things to measure. My answer to these questions is "You should spend enough to ensure that employees have the knowledge and skills they need to meet their personal, group, and organizational business goals." Throughout my career, I have almost always found that when I could make a solid business case for a training initiative, I was never denied the funds for that initiative. The key is to tie your learning initiatives directly to those business goals.

I also make the point that the training budget should not be a direct measure of the volume of learning that should be taking place within an organization. In an organization with a positive learning environment, every employee should be learning every day as part of their jobs. In my book, *Learn Your Way to Success*[5], I present a wide variety of learning opportunities and learning methods that employees can access and utilize as part of their regular jobs, over and above any specific training they receive.

Creating a Positive Learning Environment

Often, when I have given a presentation or a seminar, I have asked the audience one or both of these questions:

---

[5] McGraw-Hill, 2012

- How would you feel if your CEO walked into your office and found you reading a book?
- How would your manager respond to this request: "I'd like to spend one morning a month at the local university library reading the latest industry journals and magazines to try to find some new ideas to help us improve our operations"?

Most people respond to the first question by saying that they would be embarrassed that they were caught "not working." But if the book is related to your work, and not a romance or sci-fi novel, in an organization with a positive learning environment, the CEO might ask you what you were reading and whether it had any ideas that might be of value to the organization.

In response to the second question, most audience members say that their manager's answer would probably be: "That's a great idea, but why don't you do it on your own time. We're paying you to work, not to spend time at the library." Again, I make the point that if the organization has a PLE, the search for new ideas to improve individual, group, and overall organizational performance would be viewed as a critical part of everyone's job.

In my book, *All Learning Is Self-Directed*[6], I provide a lot of advice on how to create a positive

---
[6] ASTD, 2000

learning environment (PLE) within an organization. My definition of a PLE is as follows:

> A positive learning environment encourages, even demands, that every employee at every level be in a continuous learning mode, constantly searching for new ideas, trying new methods, sharing ideas and learning with others, and learning from others, to find new and better ways to achieve individual, group, and organizational business goals.

Creating a PLE is a vital step in ensuring that learning takes place and is valued in any organization. Getting results from investments in training and learning require the support of both formal and informal learning activities at every level of the organization.

What If…?

What if every manager in an organization, from the CEO on down, started every staff meeting with this question: "What have we learned since our last meeting that can help us improve our business results?" My guess is that the first few times the question was asked, the manager would get a lot of blank stares and very few responses. But if the manager kept asking the question at every meeting, it wouldn't be long before the staff started providing answers, and good answers at that.

The Ultimate Measure

The best compliment I ever received came from the head of the networks business unit at DEC. Upon announcing that the company had increased its networks business revenue from $400 million to more than $1 billion in less than four years, he commented: "And we couldn't have done it without Networks University."

Chapter 6

Other Lessons Learned

During my career, I have started up the training function in several companies and have been recruited to manage an existing training group in several others. I have consulted to dozens of companies and drawn stories from dozens of others in doing research for my books. In this chapter, I will provide some lessons learned on a variety of topics from my own experiences. It is my hope that you find value in at least some of these stories.

Managing a Management Education Group

The company was establishing a new management education group which would combine several different groups that existed in various parts of the company. I had been asked to head up a development group that would focus on corporate functions – engineering, manufacturing, finance, human resources, marketing, etc. A second group would focus on field-based groups, such as sales, field service, and software services. This was my first job as a manager.

I inherited six people from the groups that were being consolidated. At my first meeting with them, I introduced myself and talked about how I would like to work as their manager. I was startled by their response: "We don't believe you!" What had I done to start with such distrust? I had never met these people before, and I had no track record as a manager for them to criticize. I asked them, "Why don't you believe me?" Their response was that their previous managers had made promises to them and had never lived up to those promises, so why should they believe me?

This negative attitude was repeated in a few more meetings. After struggling with how to respond to such negativity, I decided to meet with each person individually. I told each of them "I understand that you were unhappy with your previous management. I'm not them. What I would like you to do is to air all of your grievances with how you've been managed so that I can learn from your past managers' errors. But once you have vented, I expect you to take me at my word unless I somehow violate that word. I will be careful not to repeat the mistakes your past managers have made, but if I do, I will expect you to raise the issue immediately rather than let it fester." The strategy worked and I slowly gained the trust of all but one person – that person was so troubled by past treatment that she decided to leave the company and I wished her well.

As I worked with the remaining five employees, I quickly learned their strengths and weaknesses as well as their preferred work methods and the types of programs in which they were most interested. Most of them had a background in instructional design but little background in the subject matter of management. As I built the group, I hired people with a variety of skills and knowledge. My philosophy was that by building a variety of skills and subject-matter expertise in the group, I could assign projects to teams where team members would bring to the table a variety of approaches. The manager of the other development group had a different approach – she assigned each project to one person in her group. She sometimes commented to me, and to our manager, that my people weren't working hard enough because they spent too much time talking with each other. So, who was right? Was my eclectic approach better or worse than hers? While I continued throughout my career building my groups with a wide variety of skills and knowledge, the answer is that neither approach is right or wrong – it depends on the nature of the work to be done and the skills and knowledge required for that work.

Besides the fact that my group developed some outstanding programs, I believe that my employees were more engaged and content in their work because they didn't feel alone – they felt more a part of a productive group than if they were required to work on projects alone, apart from each other.

Don't Neglect Your Own Development Needs

Too often, training managers spend so much time worrying about the development of everyone else in the company that they neglect the development needs of their staffs and themselves. Here are a few ideas on how to continuously develop your own learning and development group.

- Have your staff, and yourself, attend some of your programs. Too often, developers sit in their offices creating programs with methods and materials they feel will work well, but never go to see them in action. Attend some programs and interact with the participants. You will learn a lot about what works and what doesn't to help you create better programs in the future and improve current programs.
- For each staff meeting, I assign one person from my staff to develop the agenda for the meeting, obviously with my input. This gives them a reason to sit down with their colleagues on the team to talk about what they would like to

discuss in the meeting. I then ask the same person to facilitate the meeting, so that they develop or hone their facilitation skills.
- At each of my staff meetings, I ask one person to bring in a new instrument, an exercise, an article, or a case study they found interesting or were using in a program so that everyone could learn about it and so that the whole staff could offer feedback, learn, and share ideas, about it.
- Join local chapters of professional organizations, such as the OD Network, ATD, SHRM, etc., to share ideas with others in the field. Go to their national conferences. Pick out the sessions that focus on challenges that your group if facing. Spend time in the trade show area to see what vendors are offering.
- Subscribe to the webcasts and blogs from relevant professional organizations. Get on their discussion boards. Ask questions – people are generally very willing to share their experiences whether they relate to a particular training vendor, their use of a particular e-learning programs, their success (and challenges) in implementing a learning management system (LMS), etc.
- Read the literature! There are new books coming out every year and magazine articles and blogs galore. For books, look at on-line reviews to see what others have found of greatest value. Don't limit yourself to the literature in the

learning and development field – subscribe to the trade magazines for your company's industry and the functional journals for the business functions that your group supports.
- Use LinkedIn to build your professional network with your peers in other companies. Join relevant interest groups and monitor their discussions.

360° Assessments – a Development Tool

I had been hired by one company to design and implement a leadership development program. On my first day in the new job, I went to see my boss, the vice president of human resources, to discuss where she wanted me to begin. She told me that it was not the right time to start the program. Instead, she gave me another assignment. She handed me a 360° assessment instrument. "We paid a consultant to create this survey a couple of years ago so that we could assess the top 100 people in the company. We've never been able to do this because Larry (the CEO and founder of the company) keeps coming up with objections. I want you to go see him, figure out what he wants, and then get this done." A few hours later, I met with Larry.

"Have you seen all the emails I sent about this?" he asked me. No, I hadn't seen any of them. "I'll send you the whole file," he told me. "Read them over and see what you think about my suggestions. Then come back to see me tomorrow."

By the time I returned to my office, my in-box had 17 emails forwarded from Larry. As I read through them, I saw that he was spending a lot of time trying to come up with the "perfect" formula. Larry was a former engineering professor, and he was intent on finding the most precise formula. The assessment instrument rated people on a scale of one to five. Larry had made a bunch of suggestions, such as "If someone has been with the company for five years, we should add .12 to their composite score; if they have been with the company for more than 10 years, add .16 to the score." In all, there were 25 to 30 suggestions for adjustments to each person's score.

When I went back to his office the next day, he asked me what I thought of his suggestions. "Larry," I said, "they are all reasonable suggestions, but the thing you need to realize is that the numbers don't matter."

He was shocked by my statement. "What do you mean that the numbers don't matter?" Remember that he was an engineering professor who wanted to come up with the perfect formula.

"Let's say," I told him, "that we have the perfect formula. At the end of the process, we have weighted scores for the top 100 people in the company using this instrument and all of the modifications you have suggested. The top score among the 100 people is 4.37 and the next highest score is 4.24. Tomorrow, for whatever reason, one of your direct reports leaves the company. Are you going to look at the list of scores and say '4.37 is the top score – we'll give the job to that person'?"

"Of course not," he replied. "There's a lot more that goes into such a decision than that."

"Larry," I replied, "I agree with you. The 360° assessment is meant to identify each person's strengths and those areas in which they need improvement. It isn't a method of ranking people, but a way to identify their needs for development."

I could see the light bulb go off in his head. "Go do it," he said.

360° assessments should be used to identify learning and development needs, NOT as a performance evaluation tool. They can be very useful in identifying needs across a large population or for creating individual development plans.[7]

Ensuring Consistency Across Programs

When I began working for the American Management Association (AMA), I examined all of the programs in the AMA catalog that were targeted

---

[7] See my book, *Feeding Your Leadership Pipeline: How to Develop the Next Generation of Leaders*, co-published by Berrett-Koehler and ASTD, for a more in-depth discussion of using assessments to create individual development plans and for advice on selecting an assessment vendor.

at first-level managers, I found nine different programs. Six of those programs included some instruction on coaching skills, five had sections on performance management, five had something on communications skills, etc. In all, there were eight or nine programs in the catalog that include material on coaching skills, ranging from a one-hour discussion to a full multi-day program on the topic. Further, the various programs included half a dozen different coaching models.

I recommended that the AMA settle on one coaching model that could be taught across all of its programs in greater or lesser detail depending on the time allocation in each program. The case I made was that if a company sent a customer to one of our programs to learn coaching skills and found that their employee got great value from it, they might come back to us to ask us to offer a coaching program to many more employees in-house. If we then sold them a program that used a different coaching model, they might object that we weren't delivering what was promised. (I was not successful in this argument because many of the existing programs were already very popular and the marketing people didn't want to mess with them.)

When I headed up the development group for the internal management education group mentioned above, we had a similar challenge. Because the management education group was formed by consolidating a number of small groups around the company, in many cases those groups had different approaches to teaching the same subject. For example, different groups in the company had adopted different approaches to teaching quality principles. While they all had the same goal, they had different methodologies, different tools, and different vocabularies. This resulted in many arguments about which approach was best and many misunderstandings because the different methods used much of the same vocabulary, but many of the terms had different meanings.

Another example: I had a colleague who headed up training at a nation-wide bank. As he talked with people in different functions and locations within the banking system, he found that many different groups were doing their own training. He felt that there was a lot of duplication of effort and extra expense involved, so he set out to catalog all of the training done within the bank. His instincts were correct, and he found huge duplications of effort and expense. For example, he found that three different divisions of the bank had purchased the same training program for the company's word processing software, and that each of them had purchased a company-wide license for it. He also found that different groups within the overall bank had purchased a variety of management skills programs that used different models, vocabularies, etc.

Why are there so many different models for coaching skills, quality programs, team-building, leadership, etc.? If Dan Tobin were to go to a potential client and offer to teach its employees coaching skills, for example, and tell the client that he uses Betty Smith's excellent five-step coaching model, the client might think "If Betty Smith has this excellent model, we should probably go hire her to teach it." So, instead, Dan Tobin tells the client, "Betty Smith has a wonderful five-step coaching model. But I have found that by adding two more steps to that model, you have a much improved model – the "Tobin Seven-Step Coaching Model." If you search for courses on coaching skills, you will find models that have anywhere from three steps to 12 or more steps. All the models are different, but they are essentially the same.

What is important is that your company select one model that fits with your culture and implement it consistently across the company, so that people spend their time doing coaching rather than arguing about the best approach, and that when people move from one group to another within the company, they can expect to use the same model.

Finding Cost-Effective Solutions

Here are a few ideas from my own experience and from other companies with which I have consulted on how to save some money.

- As the training group in a small company, you may not have the resources or expertise to develop and deliver all of the training your company needs. But your company does business with many larger companies, as either their suppliers or their customers. Talk with the people in those companies. Their training groups may have programs that they would be willing to share with you at little or no cost. At various times, I have also gotten agreement from some large companies to use their training or conference facilities (free of charge) for my company's training programs. A small metal-working company won a contract to build parts for a major aircraft manufacturer. The aircraft company soon started complaining about the quality of the product they were receiving. The small company asked if the aircraft manufacturer could help them, and they got both free consulting help and training from the larger company to help them produce a better product.
- Several times in my career, I have been assigned to develop a program on a topic for which there were several well-known experts, typically consultants or business school professors. My boss would say, "Wouldn't it be great to bring in one of those experts? It would really be a morale booster, and it would really get the attention of top management to use such a well-known person." Yes, it would be great – except

for the cost. Many of these experts charge $20,000, $30,000, or more per day for their time. If your company can afford it and is willing to spend the money, that's great! But more often you will have a much more modest budget. Here's what I have done in several cases (with great success). I check the websites of some of the top business schools and find a more junior faculty member who specializes in the same subject matter. These junior faculty are usually subject matter experts and great presenters (check to see if they have taught in the business school's executive education programs) and command a much lower daily rate. I also never hire anyone unless I first get to view him or her on a video or sit in on one of his or her classes.

- Don't feel that you have to reinvent the wheel every time you get a training request. There are a number of vendors who offer pre-packaged materials on a variety of training topics. If an identified training need in your company is, for example, "Finance for Non-Financial Managers," there are any number of pre-packaged courses and materials available in the marketplace. Get a few samples and review them with the relevant executive (such as your Chief Financial Officer in this example). Will they fit the need as they currently exist? If not, can you make some modifications to the packaged materials to better fit your needs? For example, at one company I had a need for this type of financial training as part of a leadership development program. I found a very good program from a vendor. After reviewing it with my CFO, he volunteered to spend an afternoon, after the completion of the vendor's program, to work with the participants on how the material related to their jobs in the company. It was a very worthwhile experience for both the participants and the CFO.

The Use and Misuse of Competency Models

When I was vice president of design and development for the American Management Association (AMA), we created the AMA Management Development Competency Model.[8] There were already many competency models on the market, but we felt that the AMA should have its own model. The AMA model lists 67 different competencies under three categories: Knowing and Managing Oneself, Knowing and Managing Others, and Knowing and Managing the Business. The model includes representative behaviors under each competency for people in the categories of

---

[8] See Daniel R. Tobin and Margaret S. Pettingell, *The AMA Guide to Management Development*, (AMACOM, 2007) to see the complete model.

individual contributor, first-level manager, mid-level manager, and functional manager.

It is a very good model, but is it better than any other model on the market? Do I advocate that organizations that have been using other models abandon them and adopt the AMA model? The answer to both questions is "No." But I do recommend that you look at the model to see if there are any insights you can gain from it. I believe that it is a very comprehensive model, but that doesn't mean that there might be something missing. At the same time, remember that there are no "secret competencies" that one company has and that no one else knows about.

Sixty-seven different competencies! Do you want to use all of them in creating job descriptions or doing performance reviews? If you try to create a hiring profile using the full model, you will find it impossible to find new employees. If you try to use all 67 competencies to do a performance review, it is unlikely that even your best employees will shine, or even have them all. Should your training group provide training to employees on each and every competency? Of course not! So how can you use such a model? What is its value?

The answer is that you should review the competencies to see which ones are most important to your organization and which fit best with your culture. Some of the competencies should be used to screen candidates, rather than becoming part of your training curriculum. For example, I don't believe that you can teach integrity – a person is either honest or not. If you think you can hire dishonest people and train them to become honest, you are deluding yourself. Similarly, I don't think you can train someone to develop charisma. Rather, focus on the skills and behaviors that are most important to the organization.

The real benefit that comes from introducing this type of competency model in your organization comes from the discussion of which competencies are most important for your organization. What are the key competencies you want the organization to hold most dear, that will distinguish it from other organizations? What type of culture do you want your organization to have? There is no one "right" culture – in many industries there will be very successful companies that have very different cultures. Taking the time to hold these discussions, not just within the training group but across the company, can yield great benefit to everyone.

Creating an Organization's Culture

Defining your organization's culture and values is important, but only if the activity is followed up by actions that support that definition. I am reminded of two stories that I have told in earlier books.

A company's senior vice president of sales and marketing was in town and requested that the regional sales manager meet with him at breakfast at his hotel. "We're cutting down on expenses. Your sales reps can no longer use their expense accounts to pay for customer meals" he told the regional manager. The manager replied, "You are staying in a suite at the most expensive hotel in the city. We're having a breakfast that will probably cost $75 or more. And you are telling me that my sales reps can't spend $25 or $30 to buy lunch for a good customer? Your actions are speaking so loudly that I can't hear a word you are saying."

The second story came from a small biotech company. The CEO had invested a lot of time and effort surveying employees to develop a set of values that would define the company's culture. Once the project was done, every employee got a plaque that displayed those values, and the plaques got put on bookshelves or in desk drawers to collect dust. More than a year later, the company had a bad result. One of its two major development projects had made it through the animal testing phase with great results and had moved on to human trials, only to discover the drug had a terrible side effect that had not shown up in the animal trials. In fact, the side effect was so bad that the company decided to shut down the human trials and abandon the development effort. The project employed almost 40 percent of the company's staff and as soon as the shutdown announcement was made, everyone feared that they or a colleague would be out of work.

The next day, the CEO called an all-company meeting in the ballroom of a hotel next door to company headquarters. Everyone came, and everyone was afraid of what would be announced. The CEO got up to speak. He held up the plaque with the company's values. "One of our key values in this company is that 'We honor great science.' The people who have been working on this project have practiced great science – the results from the human trials could not have been predicted. We come here today to honor this team. Everyone will be assigned to new projects and no one will lose their jobs." All of a sudden, those plaques got dusted off because they now had meaning.

Engaging Employees

When I founded Digital Equipment Corporation's (DEC) Networks University, my boss, the group's marketing director, told me that he wanted me to find some way of creating a unique culture for the participants. We were bringing together groups in the company that had not traditionally worked well together and he wanted to find a way of making them all feel like they belonged to a unique group – the "networks team."

DEC had a long history of providing logo-emblazoned paraphernalia to its employees. Over my 11 years with the company, I lost track of the number of t-shirts, polo shirts, dress shirts, hats, jackets, notebooks, luggage, etc., that I had accumulated. Yes, we provided those things to the participants, but he wanted something more – an experience that would be unique to the Networks University participants and not shared by anyone else in the company.

As explained earlier, the Networks University program was unique in its design, not just for DEC, but also for the computer industry as a whole (I heard this from many participants who had come from other computer companies). I called it a "learning event" rather than a training program because the informal learning that took place during each event probably exceeded that of the formal sessions we planned, and the learning was going in two directions, from corporate groups to the field, but just as importantly from the field to the corporate groups. When people walked into a hotel or conference center where Networks University was taking place, they could feel the energy in the air.

So, what could I do that would provide a unique experience? I took a risk. At the program's fifth session, I announced a guest speaker for the Thursday evening dinner. Dr. Gene Taylor from the

National Bureau of Standards was introduced as the speaker who would discuss national and international networking standards. He was introduced by the person who worked on those standards for our company. Everyone was impressed by Dr. Taylor's biography as read in the introduction.

National and international networking standards may be among the most boring topics ever included in the Networks University agenda. And the speaker was speaking at the Thursday evening dinner, when everyone in the room (about 600 people) had been overworked for the entire week. During the week, a number of the participants had already complained to me about having such a boring topic after the dinner. I told them to be patient, I thought they would get a lot out of the presentation.

Only three people (my meeting planner, the person who would introduce the speaker, and another person who worked for me), besides myself, knew that the presentation was a hoax. I had hired a double-talk artist to play the role of Dr. Taylor. I had given him two pages of buzzwords from the networking lexicon and a two-page overview of networking standards to work with.

At dinner, my meeting planner was seated next to my boss (who didn't know that the speaker wasn't genuine). Unfortunately, she was unaware that he didn't know, and she commented to him that "this guy's going to be a riot." Immediately, my boss said he wanted to meet with me outside the ballroom. He asked what was going to happen and I told him the plan. "You know," he said, "you've had an extremely successful week, and you just might ruin it all with this stunt." "Trust me," I said nervously.

Dr. Taylor got up and started stringing together buzzwords that made no sense at all. After a couple of minutes, people in the audience started getting antsy. He then read one of the paragraphs from the briefing document that did make sense, and people settled down. He then went back to the buzzwords, every few minutes interjecting something that made sense. And, as he went on, he became more and more outrageous, until people were laughing loudly. "I started working for the government during the Carter administration. You remember the Carter administration? It was in all the papers." After 15 minutes, he exposed the hoax and spent time talking about his experiences working as a hoax artist. My boss was laughing so hard that he actually fell off his chair. At the end of the dinner, he came to me and said, "That's the kind of risk I want you to take."

Move ahead 25 years. The company for which I was working had just hired a new vice president of sales. I saw in the announcement that she had once worked for DEC, and her name was vaguely familiar. I stopped by her office to introduce myself and welcome her to the company. "You did Networks University!" she exclaimed. "That was the best program I ever attended. I don't think that

I've ever felt more a part of a group than when I attended Networks U. Do you remember Dr. Gene Taylor?"

There are many ways to build employee engagement. Find one that works for your organization.

Beware of Bells and Whistles

When I worked as a training director and as a corporate university dean, I was constantly besieged by vendors who offered the latest and greatest tools and programs. The proliferation of e-learning tools, LMS platforms, and training programs continues apace. While it may be tempting to be on the cutting edge and to show everyone that your training group has the latest technology, beware of getting so enamored of the technology and all its bells and whistles that you lose sight of your basic mission. Here are a few stories from my own experience.

- In the early days of e-learning, back around the turn of the century, I received a sample CD from a start-up e-learning company. The topic was "change management." The company had recruited an impressive array of business school professors to provide papers and mini-lectures on the topic, and both the list of presenters and the content were notable.

    When I loaded the CD into my PC, it brought up a cartoon-like drawing of a town square. The directions were to enter the library building to read articles and to enter the theater to hear lectures. I entered the theater. From the menu, I chose a presentation from a noted business school professor. On the theater's stage, the professor's talking head appeared atop a small cartoon-depiction of a robot and proceeded to give his lecture on the topic. While the lecture was going on, the background on the stage turned into a light-and-laser show. The show was so impressive that I barely heard the lecture.

- I had hired a well-known media company to create a slide set for a customer seminar. When I got the slides back, there were several sequences that built bulleted lists. The background for these slides looked like a jigsaw puzzle where each piece of the puzzle was a different color. This would have been distracting enough, but as the slide sat on the screen, the pieces kept changing colors so that it was nearly impossible to concentrate on the content being presented.
- I got a disc from a company from Australia that focused on team-building skills. It was very well done, containing video scenarios demonstrating common problems and then showing how to overcome those problems.

While the disk was self-paced, the package also contained an instructor guide with instructions on how to use the videos in a live classroom setting and offered additional materials that could be used in a live class. It was one of the best packages I had seen and I used it extensively with great success. A couple of years later, the Australian company was bought by an American e-learning company. This company converted the package to their on-line learning platform. In doing so, they replaced the videos with still photos while keeping the audio portions. They also eliminated the instructor guide. And, from my point of view, they destroyed much of the value of the original package.

- Over the years, I have participated in many simulations, ranging from simple board games to sophisticated computer simulations. They can be very entertaining and engaging and a lot of learning can come from them. But beware! Sometimes, and too often, participants remember more how much fun they had, rather than the learning objectives of the experience. You need to structure these types of experiences so that the learning objectives are at the forefront and, as people participate in the games, you remind them of what they are learning.

Overcoming Obstacles to Build a New Business

In my last couple of years at DEC, I worked as an executive education director for the company's marketing vice president. One day, people came to me with this problem to solve. The company had decided to start a management consulting business and had hired two dozen experienced consultants from several major management consulting firms. The problem was that these high-priced consultants weren't able to get meetings with customer executives. The sales reps for major accounts didn't understand the new business or what these consultants did, and they were afraid to put them in front of their customers for fear that they might lose control of these large accounts. Could I come up with a way of getting these consultants into these accounts?

Digital's sales organization had a long history of sponsoring executive education programs for CEOs and other senior business executives. The company would hire a well-known consultant or business school professor to put on a two-day seminar on some topic they felt would interest the target audience. The sales reps would invite senior executives to the seminars, always based at a luxury resort or conference center.

The strategy worked in terms of attracting the right level of executives, but these seminars rarely led to any new business. There were a couple of problems with the strategy. First, DEC's sales reps dealt almost exclusively with companies' technical staffs – from information technology departments certainly, but also from the companies' scientists and engineers who used DEC's equipment. They could talk "computer-speak" but not the language of the business. This recognition led to the second problem: because the sales reps were not knowledgeable about the business topics being covered in the seminars, they were not allowed to attend the seminars with their customers. They could sit in another room and watch the presentation via a video feed, but DEC feared that if they were in the same room, they would demonstrate their ignorance on the topics being discussed. The sales reps' sole assignment once they got the executives to attend was to take them to an expensive dinner at the end of the first day of the seminar.

Here's the solution to these problems that I came up with.

- First, we needed a topic for a seminar that would utilize the skills of the management consultants and, at the same time, suggest how DEC's technology could be used to enable and facilitate a solution to the executive's business challenges. Based on extensive talks with the management consulting staff, we chose the topic: "Creating an Adaptive Organization." After selecting the topic and outlining the full details of the

program, we asked sales reps to recruit a customer, at the level of a "vice-president and division general manager" of a Fortune 100 customer. We got 11 takers.
- Second, we needed a way to get the sales reps and the management consultants to work together *before* the seminar was held. We also needed to educate the sales reps on the topic so that they could intelligently participate in the seminar and subsequent discussions with the customer executives. I hired a business school professor to give the two-day seminar. The twist was that we would give the seminar twice, first to an audience of sales reps and the management consultants we paired with each sales rep and, *two months later*, to the executive audience, with the management consultants and sales reps sitting with their customers.
- Third, in the two-month interval between the two seminars, the sales rep and the assigned management consultant had to interview the customer and four or more of the customer's direct reports, about his/her organizational challenges. From these interviews and from the content of the seminar they had already attended, they were to develop a discussion agenda that they would use with the customer at the executive seminar.
- We then held the two-day seminar for the customer executives. On the morning following

the seminar, the sales rep and the management consultant sat with the customer to discuss: "Here's what we heard in the seminar and here's what we heard from you and your direct reports. Now, here are some ways that we think we can help you. What do you think?"
- The final step was that within two weeks after the executive seminar, each sales rep and management consultant pair were to meet with the customer to present a proposal of how they could help the customer.

Of the eleven customers who attended the seminar, seven signed contracts based on those proposals. All four of the sales reps who were not successful with their proposals told us that the seminar (1) helped them break into their customer's senior executive ranks much more quickly than they could have done on their own, and (2) helped them understand the role of the management consultants so that they would use them to help with future proposals.

A Final Word

While I realize that not every idea in this book will be new to readers and that not everyone will agree with the approaches I have built, my hope is that the people who read this book will get at least some ideas that might help them with their organizational learning efforts.

For further information on any of the topics, please refer to my previously published books listed elsewhere in this book.

I would greatly enjoy hearing from readers about what they found most stimulating from this book and how specific ideas may have changed their thinking or given them new ideas on how to approach the challenges they face in their jobs every day.

Books by Daniel R. Tobin

Learn Your Way to Success, McGraw-Hill, 2012

Feeding Your Leadership Pipeline, Berrett-Kohler and ASTD, 2010

The AMA Guide to Management Development (with Margaret Pettingell), AMACOM, 2008

All Learning Is Self-Directed: How Organizations Can Support and Encourage Independent Learning, ASTD, 2000

The Knowledge-Enabled Organization: Moving from Training to Learning to Meet Business Goals, AMACOM, 1997

Transformational Learning: Renewing Your Company Through Knowledge and Skills, John Wiley & Sons, 1996

Re-Educating the Corporation: Foundations for the Learning Organization, John Wiley & Sons, 1994

About Dan Tobin

Dan Tobin has spent all of his 72 years learning. He has been in the education/learning/ talent development/training profession for 51 of those years, starting as a junior high school math teacher after graduating from college. Following four years of teaching math, he returned to graduate school at Cornell University, earning a master's degree in public administration and a Ph.D. in the economics of education. While at Cornell, he was employed in the university's planning office and as a researcher at the Cornell Institute for Adult and Occupational Education. From there, he became director of research and planning at Quinsigamond Community College in Massachusetts.

In 1981, he moved from academia to industry, working 11 years at Digital Equipment Corporation where, among other assignments, he founded Digital's Networks University, a global program unique in the computer industry. After Digital, he worked as an independent consultant, speaker, and author on corporate learning strategies until taking a job to found Wang Global Virtual University. Dan has also worked for a start-up dot-com company which burst with the dot-com bubble and as director of employee development and organizational learning for Aspen Technology, Inc. Dan's last full-time job was as vice president of program design and development for the American Management Association (AMA). Since leaving the AMA, he has worked as an independent consultant, speaker, and author.

Dan is the author of seven previous books on corporate learning strategies (listed elsewhere). He has given keynotes and workshops on five continents. He resides in White Plains, New York, and can be reached at dantobin2016@gmail.com.

www.ingramcontent.com/pod-product-compliance
Lightning Source LLC
Chambersburg PA
CBHW032001170526
45157CB00002B/492